I have just completed reading the book *Walk with Me*, and it is so good that I want to start immediately to read it again! It has a unique approach—one that I thoroughly enjoyed. I recommend this book to readers of all ages as it not only inspires us and makes us more knowledgeable in the Scriptures, but is interesting and fun to read as well.

—**Gene Stallings**
Head Football Coach
University of Alabama

HEAR MY VOICE.
WATCH MY ACTIONS.
FOLLOW MY STEPS. COME...

WALK
with Me

PRENTICE A. MEADOR, JR.
AND BOB G. CHISHOLM

Regal Books
A Division of Gospel Light
Ventura, California, U.S.A.

Published by Regal Books
A Division of GL Publications
Ventura, CA 93006
Printed in U.S.A.

Library of Congress Cataloging-in-Publication Data
Meador, Prentice, 1938-
Walk with Me / Prentice A. Meador, Jr., Bob G. Chisholm.
p. cm.
ISBN 0-8307-1436-7
1. Bible. N.T. Mark—Meditations. I. Chisholm, Bob, 1953-
II. Title.
BS2585.4.M42 1990
242'.5—dc20

90-41245
CIP

2 3 4 5 6 7 8 9 / KP / X3.0 / 95 94 93 92

Rights for publishing this book in other languages are contracted by Gospel Literature International (GLINT) foundation. GLINT also provides technical help for the adaptation, translation, and publishing of Bible study resources and books in scores of languages worldwide. For further information, contact GLINT, Post Office Box 488, Rosemead, California, 91770, U.S.A., or the publisher.

Dedicated
to
the people of
Red Bridge Church of Christ
Kansas City, Missouri
and
Prestoncrest Church of Christ
Dallas, Texas

Contents

8

Oppose Me

"Jesus' determination put Him on a collision course with the religious establishment. Religion's categories had grown hard. Its leadership and direction had become a burden to the purposes of God. And so, conflict was unavoidable."

83

9

Believe Me

"Jesus was saying, 'You believed in Me when it was easy, when it was popular, when it was exciting. But will you believe in Me now, knowing more of the story? Will you believe in Me when it's hard?'"

93

10

Pray with Me

"Jesus too had the choice of right or wrong. He too stood in the gap between loyalty and betrayal, integrity and hypocrisy. And for Him, the distance between a good decision and a bad one was measured in units of prayer."

103

11

Suffer with Me

"Because He was painfully aware of His own suffering, Jesus had a special right to speak. Especially did He have this right when He explained to His disciples that they will suffer."

113

12
Remember Me

"We keep His memory alive because He is alive. And so, we encounter Jesus, not because He is more present in the Supper than at any other time, but because, in the Supper, we are more aware."

123

13
Preach Me

"On the other side of His death, Jesus prepared the Twelve to sow the 'many seeds' of His resurrection. He prepared them to preach."

133

1

Follow Me

Imagine that you are a Jew living in a small Palestinian village in the year A.D. 30. In the village is a synagogue, where, ever since your childhood, your elders have told you stories of your heritage and your faith—the patriotic history of your nation.

The storytellers spoke of "the good old days" when Israel soared to her peak. She was the greatest, the richest, the biggest—the chosen nation of God. He gave her wealth, power and those great leaders that you long for today: Saul, Solomon, David—especially David, the warrior king, yet "a man after [God's] own heart" (1 Sam. 13:14).

But the storytellers also recounted the tale of Israel's fall. A thousand years ago she began to lose her great unity. You suffered as the elders told of the split into two kingdoms. You wept at hearing how the Assyrians erased the Northern Kingdom from the earth. It grieved you to hear of the Babylonian conquest of the Southern Kingdom.

"Why!" you wondered. "We were the best! We were the strongest! We were God's chosen people!"

As your heritage was unfolded, you began to see a painful pattern. Israel was passed from one conqueror to another. The good old days began to fade in your mind as you were told how your people were passed from Babylonia to Persia, from Persia to Greece and from Greece to Syria. You feel the pain and share the grief of generations. You see old men cry and others burn with anger. Frustration too? And shame? Yes, all that and worse.

They described how large numbers of your people were sold into slavery. You felt their emotion as they told how the Temple was plundered. December 15, 168 B.C. is a hole torn in the heart of Israel. For on this day the heathen god Zeus was placed on the altar of the Temple. Ten days later a pig was sacrificed there. It is a hole torn in your heart.

Hope flickered, if only for a moment, as the elders told of Maccabean victories. They spoke with admiration of the Jewish families who fought back trying to regain the good old days. But today's reality is Rome. Can Rome be overthrown? You have hope.

Some have given up, but you remember the promise: *"One day a great leader will return."* The old men said, "He will regain what has been lost. He will unify the nation. He will crush our enemies."

Will this great leader be another Moses? Will it be Elijah coming back? Or how about Jeremiah? Or does it really matter?

What counts is the Kingdom. It must be restored. We must have the Messiah.

Many share your faith. Many are willing to fight. The expectations are so strong that many have already come, claiming to be the Messiah: Judas, son of Hezekiah, who led a revolt in Galilee. Simon, a former royal servant, proclaimed king in Perea. Athronges of Judea, the shepherd-king willing to attack the Romans. Judas of Galilee, founder of the Zealots. The imposter Theudas and others.

All promised a military answer to centuries of repression. All stirred the political hopes of the people. All said, "Follow me."

Many Jews did, and many died.

And now today in A.D. 30, another man appears in the nearby wilderness. He is powerful, not afraid to confront King Herod. "Adulterer!" cries John the Baptist. And he goes to prison for it. Is John our leader, our Messiah?

"No," John says, "another comes after me." He points to "one more powerful, the thongs of whose sandals I am not worthy to stoop down and untie" (Mark 1:7).

At this point Jesus steps into the picture. When you see Him you see authority and control. You see awesome power and wisdom.

But what does it all mean? What do you, the first-century Jew, conclude? Who is Jesus and why has He come?

With this background and with the heart and hopes of first-century Palestine, consider now the first time that Jesus said, "Follow me."

> After John was put in prison, Jesus went into Galilee, proclaiming the good news of God.
>
> "The time has come," he said. "The kingdom of God is near. Repent and believe the good news!"
>
> As Jesus walked beside the Sea of Galilee, he saw Simon and his brother Andrew casting a net into the lake, for they were fishermen.
>
> "Come, follow me," Jesus said, "and I will make you fishers of men."
>
> At once they left their nets and followed Him.
>
> When he had gone a little farther, he saw James son of Zebedee and his brother John in a boat, preparing their nets. Without delay he called them, and they left their father Zebedee in the boat with

the hired men and followed him (Mark 1:14-20).

What did Jesus mean when He said, "Follow me"? Should we assume that when His first disciples heard Him say, "Follow me," they automatically thought, *This is the Son of God! We are going to write the Bible. We are going to teach our people how to love their enemies. We are going to establish the Church"?*

There is really no valid reason for us to give these twentieth-century viewpoints to a first-century encounter. But there is every reason to think that a first-century Jew would see Jesus as his long-awaited political Messiah. The political longing had existed much too long.

So when Jesus said, "Follow me," Simon, Andrew, James and John dropped their nets and followed, but not entirely for the right reasons. Their political motives were ambitious and self-serving, yet Jesus allowed them. He did not say, "Your motivation must be absolutely pure. Your understanding must be entirely accurate. You must know exactly who I am and what I have come here to do or you can't follow Me."

He simply said, "Follow me." He allowed them to follow for the wrong reasons because He knew correction would take time.

His patience is impressive. He entered the world going in an opposite direction, and His job was to turn the human race around. How did He do it? Patiently—one person at a time. This is why Jesus chose to concentrate on 12 disciples.

If Jesus had wanted to infuse those disciples miraculously with instant understanding, instant maturity and instant commitment, He could have. He could have done it with millions. He could have changed everyone's mind instantly.

But He could have done so only by violating their freedom and their power of choice. And Jesus wanted their choice. He wanted their decision. So He simply said, "Follow me."

Jesus took people as they were—politically charged,

nationalistically motivated, but willing to follow. And the meaning of following Jesus was gradually unfolded to them. He did not tell them all at once. He told them in as much depth and in as much quantity as they could accept.

As Mark said, "Jesus spoke the word to them, as much as they could understand" (4:33). He did this because they could not grasp it all. He hoped they would have "ears to hear" (4:9,23), knowing that the vast majority would not. And so He chose 12, hoping they would finally give Him their choice.

Is your business more important than your faith? Your hobby more important than your worship?

And by allowing freedom, Jesus allowed struggle. First, the Twelve struggled with Him. He wasn't what they had expected.

One day Jesus calmed a storm on the Sea of Galilee (4:35-41). The Twelve watched Him bring it to a sudden halt, and His doing so scared them. His feat was much larger than the political category to which they had consigned Him. Their words, "Who is this?" were another way of saying, "He is not who we thought He was."

When Jesus announced for the first time that He would have to die, Peter struggled (8:31-32). He fought it and rebuked Jesus, as if to say, "You are *not* going to die. That's not the way it works."

The Twelve "did not understand...and were afraid to ask" (9:32). They had been with Him a long time, but still did not understand. They struggled with Him.

But, at the same time, He struggled with them:

- Don't you understand? (4:13)
- Why are you so afraid? (4:40)
- Are you so dull?...Don't you see? (7:18)
- Do you still not see or understand? Are your hearts hardened? (8:17)
- Do you have eyes but fail to see, and ears but fail to hear? And don't you remember? (8:18)
- Do you still not understand? (8:21)

From this message, "Follow me," come important lessons describing what it means for us to follow Jesus today:

FOLLOW ME INSTEAD OF SOMEONE ELSE

The alternatives for the Twelve are not all that different from our own. Politics, power, wealth, success, pleasure—these alternatives compete for our allegiance today. They all say, "Follow me."

Is your business more important than your faith? Is your hobby more important than your worship? Are your possessions more important than your soul?

These questions are relevant for us today. Yet they were composed in the first century. Just as He did then, Jesus asks us today to follow Him instead of something or someone else.

FOLLOW ME FROM WHERE YOU ARE

Those early followers did not come to Jesus neutral or perfect. They came with problems and flaws. But Jesus took them as they were. And He began to change them at the very point where He met them. To be sure, they were stubborn and selfish, but He stayed with them and worked with them.

This is how Jesus relates to us when we are stubborn and when we fail. He doesn't ask us to wait until we have our lives all put together before we follow. He asks us to follow Him from where we are right now.

FOLLOW ME TO MY DESTINATION

Much later in the story things became tense. Many began to leave Jesus after discovering that He would not accept a political kingship. Jesus asked His original followers, "You do not want to leave too, do you?" (John 6:67).

Jesus asks us today to follow Him instead of something or someone else.

Their answer was, "To whom shall we go?" (6:68).

The point is powerful: If we stay with Jesus long enough, it will become clear to us that we have no other alternative. All other promises are hollow and lead nowhere.

Jesus did describe another way. But, He said, it is "wide" and leads to "destruction" (Matt. 7:13). Yet we need not go that way. We can stay with Him and follow Him all the way to His destination—all the way to heaven.

FOLLOW ME IN MY MISSION

We can only guess what the Twelve thought of Jesus' original call, "Follow me,...and I will make you fishers of men" (Mark 1:17). He certainly knew they did not understand. But if they would stay with Him, they would later look back on these early words with a clearer understanding.

So it is with us. Our initial efforts at ministry are awkward and simplistic, perhaps even rigid and legalistic. But the longer we follow Him, the more we will go about our ministry as He did—with patience and service.

So when Mark closes His story with the final command, "Go" (16:15), we must put it in the framework of Jesus' ministry. The Great Commission is not a generic motivational formula; rather, it is the final statement of a story that gives it its meaning and style. Many are the ways to engage in a religious mission, but Jesus asks us to follow *Him* in *His* mission.

FOR REFLECTION

1. What is the historical background of Israel from David to Jesus?

2. What did some of the disciples think Jesus meant by "follow me"?

3. Why did Jesus not give His disciples instant maturity, understanding and commitment?

4. How did the apostles struggle with what it really means to follow Jesus?

5. Who or what are you most tempted to follow instead of Jesus?

6. In what ways do church people sometimes say to the world, "Clean up your life, then follow Jesus"? How is Jesus' method different?

7. How do we, like the apostles, try to make Jesus into someone else?

8. What are some practical ways that I can improve my own personal following of Jesus?

9. What does it mean to be involved in the mission of Jesus?

10. What are the practical implications of following Jesus in:

> your family?
>
> your business?
>
> nonchurch relationships?
>
> within the church?

2

Understand Me

- He was despised and rejected by men, a man of sorrows, and familiar with suffering (Isa. 53:3).
- For I endure scorn for your sake, and shame covers my face. I am a stranger to my brothers, an alien to my own mother's sons (Ps. 69:7-8).

These two texts from the Old Testament introduce Jesus Christ. But they are not the kind of introductions we might expect for the Lord of lords. We would expect the King of kings to be loved, admired and understood, but these verses speak of His *not* being known by His brothers and *not* being welcome in His mother's house. Of all the sorrows of Jesus, one cut particularly deep: the sorrow of family misunderstanding.

Ever since He was a young boy, Jesus' mother had watched Him, storing up the events in her heart (see Luke 2:51). Gradually an understanding gap began to develop in the family. It can be seen as early as 12 years of age, when Jesus stayed behind at the Temple. This move toward independence caused particular anxiety when His parents realized that He was not with them. After they searched and found him, their discussion reveals the misunderstanding:

> "Why were you searching for me?" he asked. "Didn't you know I had to be in my Father's house?"
> But they did not understand what he was saying to them (Luke 2:49-50).

Jesus continued to mature into manhood and His sense of mission became more concrete. So when He finally began His public ministry His teaching and His actions became even more difficult for His family to understand.

> Then Jesus entered a house, and again a crowd gathered, so that he and his disciples were not even able to eat. When his family heard about this, they went to take charge of him, for they said, "He is out of his mind"....
> Then Jesus' mother and brothers arrived. Standing outside, they sent someone in to call him. A crowd was sitting around him, and they told him, "Your mother and brothers are outside looking for you."
> "Who are my mother and my brothers?" he asked.
> Then he looked at those seated in a circle around him and said, "Here are my mother and my brothers! Whoever does God's will is my brother and sister and mother" (Mark 3:20-21,31-35).

The pain Jesus felt was not inflicted by a worldly crowd, by jealous Pharisees or even by stubborn disciples. This pain came from His family. Having heard that He had gone insane, they had come to "take charge" of the situation (vs. 21). In the original language, the word is "seize."

We can only guess what His family was thinking. They had heard the rumors. And they must have been asking themselves, "What does all this mean?"

Finally His mother and brothers could no longer ignore the answer to that question. They had been hearing about Jesus' behavior for a long time. The rumors were ugly, but

---

When Jesus came into the world, He found one vortex for human life: self.... Jesus refused to be pulled into this swirl. Instead He humbled Himself and became a servant. No wonder Jesus looked odd and eccentric.

---

they finally had to face them. Jesus had gone crazy. He was out of His mind. He simply was not responsible for what He was doing.

And so, as they moved into the crowd, we can almost hear them apologizing for Jesus: "Never mind about Jesus. He is beside Himself. We will talk to Him and take Him home."

Even when they are true, these are awful things to say. But they are even more awful when they are not true. And they become unbearable when they come from those whose support and understanding we desperately want—those who are our own flesh and blood.

How much Jesus must have wanted His family to understand Him. John 1:11 states, "He came to that which was his own, but his own did not receive him."

Why is this story here? What is there to learn from it? Consider these lessons:

THE CHARGES AGAINST JESUS WERE TRUE

From the world's standpoint, the accusations against Jesus were accurate. The word that is translated "he is out of his mind" literally means "to stand outside of—to be beside oneself—to be eccentric." Jesus *was* eccentric. His center was in a different place.

When Jesus came into the world, He found one vortex for human life: self. The circle around that center was called selfishness, and everyone traveled in it. Jesus refused to be pulled into this swirl of selfishness. Instead He did curious things like humbling Himself and becoming a servant (see Phil. 2:5-8). No wonder Jesus looked odd and eccentric.

Satan could find nothing in the center of Jesus' life to twist or corrupt because Jesus stood outside the center of His life. Something else was at His core. He identifies it with the words, "Whoever does God's will"(Mark 3:35).

John recorded similar words from Jesus:

- My food...is to do the will of him who sent me and to finish his work (John 4:34).
- By myself I can do nothing;...I seek not to please myself but him who sent me (5:30).
- I have come...not to do my will but to do the will of him who sent me (6:38).
- I do nothing on my own but speak just what the Father has taught me (8:28).
- The world must learn that...I do exactly what my Father has commanded me (14:31).

Jesus had one center around which His life revolved, one

source of nourishment—the Father's will. And so there was misunderstanding because Jesus' life was unusual. It was odd. And the charges against Him were true. He *was* eccentric. He *did* have a different center.

> *From the world's standpoint, true Christianity continues to be eccentric.... Even the language used in the New Testament to describe the Christian life sounds exaggerated to everyone except those who have experienced a new life.*

LIVING LIKE JESUS PRODUCES THE SAME REACTION

Selfishness is still the center of the world, and following Jesus will still bring scoffing and scorn. In one of His last recorded prayers, Jesus said:

> I have given them your word and the world has hated them, for they are not of the world any more than I am of the world. My prayer is not that you take them out of the world but that you protect them from the evil one....As you sent me into the world, I have sent them into the world (John 17:14,15,18).

Two chapters earlier He had said:

> If the world hates you, keep in mind that it hated me first. If you belonged to the world, it would love you as its own. As it is, you do not belong to the world,

> but I have chosen you out of the world. That is why
> the world hates you. Remember the words I spoke to
> you: "No servant is greater than his master." If they
> persecuted me, they will persecute you also (John
> 15:18-20).

From the world's standpoint, true Christianity *continues* to be eccentric. It continues to be off-center from the rest of the population. The broad way and the narrow way are still at right angles to each other. They revolve around different centers and spin in opposite directions. Even the language used in the New Testament to describe the Christian life sounds exaggerated to everyone except those who have experienced a new birth, a new life, a new heart, a new center, a new direction.

Much later in his own life, Peter describes the reaction of old associates to this new life and this new center. "They think it strange that you do not plunge with them into the same flood of dissipation" (1 Pet. 4:4). He is referring to the flood of "debauchery, lust, drunkenness, orgies, carousing and detestable idolatry" (v. 3).

The old crowd will retaliate when we move out of their circle. They will "heap abuse on you" (v. 4). The Eastern proverb applies: "The nail that sticks out usually gets hammered down."

And so the Christian businessman is thought of as odd because he will not go out after work drinking with everyone else. The Christian waitress is called prudish by her boss because she refuses to wear immodest clothing in his restaurant. A Christian young man is laughed at because he skips a school function to go to worship.

A successful Christian photographer loses her job because she refuses to do a pornographic layout for a client. A Christian man is criticized by his accountant because his church contribution is so large he cannot write all of it off on his taxes. He is called foolish and stupid. A Christian couple is ridiculed by three rows of movie-goers because they leave a movie that has gone past their values.

These people are not arrogant. They don't rub their faith in your face. Peter wrote, "If you suffer, it should not be as a murderer or a thief or any other kind of criminal, or even as a meddler" (1 Pet. 4:15).

These people are not meddlers. They are simply choosing God over everything else. They are bearing the legitimate reproach of the cross.

If the life-style of Jesus brought His death, why should we not expect discomfort? A new center that brings peace with God very often does *not* bring peace with anyone else.

One of the most distressing observations from reading the Gospels is the narrowing of Jesus' relationships. The story begins with crowds and popularity, but as the message becomes clearer, people begin to lose patience. The crowds thin out. The applause dies down.

Jesus is questioned, accused, ignored, slandered and certainly misunderstood. Eventually, many of His disciples leave Him. Soon there are only 12. Then 11. And finally only one—one who denies that he even knows Jesus.

TURN TO THE CENTER OF YOUR FAITH

What do you do when your faith is misunderstood? What do you do when you have to choose between the approval of God and the approval of friends, family and work associates? Where do you turn when you go to your own and they do not receive you? Consider again Jesus' words:

"Who are my mother and my brothers?" he asked. Then he looked at those seated in a circle around him and said, "Here are my mother and my brothers! Whoever does God's will is my brother and sister and mother" (Mark 3:33-35).

First, notice that Jesus turned to His center—the will of God. Often, there is no other place to turn. The Gospel of Mark reports Jesus praying three times (1:35; 6:46; 14:32-42). And all three were occasions of crisis—three times when there was no other place to turn, three times when there was no human support, three times when no one understood. So He turned to someone who did understand. He turned to the will of God. Where do you turn?

Second, He also had a human support group. Jesus considered them His family: "Whoever does God's will is my brother and sister and mother" (Mark 3:35). His group included others who were also off-center, also traveling in another orbit.

Those in our human support group are called the Church. The center of their lives is the same as ours. They too revolve around the will of God.

Jesus, pointing to those in the circle around Him, was saying, "Here is my real family. Here are the ones who understand what the center of life ought to be."

Are you a part of such a group? Do you have a human support group who shares with you the real center of life? Do you have such a "family"?

The decision to turn to the will of God and to the people of God is the same decision. It is a decision to be *off-center* but, at the same time, *on-course.*

FOR REFLECTION

1. How did Jesus differ from the expectations of so many people?

2. Describe the gap that began to develop between Jesus and His family?

3. In what ways did Jesus' family totally misunderstand Him?

4. In what sense was Jesus an "eccentric"?

5. How does persecution today differ from the first century?

6. What were the human responses to the teaching and life of Jesus? Why?

7. How is it true that every person who lives like Jesus will produce the same reaction in people?

8. What is the difference between having a different center and simply being irritable and arrogant?

9. Give examples of how peace with God often does not bring peace with the world.

10. What are three practical steps you can take to prepare for the misunderstandings that will come from those in or out of the Church?

3

Listen to Me

Oh, be careful little eyes what you see....
Oh, be careful little ears what you hear....
Oh, be careful little tongue what you say....
Oh, be careful little hands what you do....
Oh, be careful little feet where you go....[1]

This is a children's song, but not exclusively so. It contains an adult message as profound as "Jesus Loves Me," another so-called children's song. Of the important principles that Jesus taught, one of the most comprehensive and yet, overlooked was simply "Be careful little ears what you hear." Or, to use Jesus words, "Consider carefully what you hear" (Mark 4:24).

Literally, this phrase means "*See* what you hear." In other words, pay close attention to it. Reflect on it. Give it some time and thought. Jesus' words were a solemn reminder of the responsibility of hearing.

Actually, Jesus was not the first to give hearing a preeminent position. The Old Testament elevates it over the other senses. Notice, for example, the process that qualified priests for God's service:

> Take the other ram....Slaughter it, take some of its
> blood and *put it on the lobes of the right ears* of Aaron
> and his sons (Exod. 29:19,20, emphasis added).

We might expect the eyes to be anointed to see God or the tongue to be anointed to proclaim God. But more fundamental than seeing or proclaiming, the ears were anointed so they could hear God and take His message deep inside. The ear was so important in the total picture of a person, that it became a symbol for the human being. And so the literal Hebrew phrase, "before the ears," translated "in the hearing" (Gen. 23:10) really meant "before me."

It's no wonder then that Isaiah would say that God revealed himself "in my hearing" (Isa. 22:14), or that each morning God "wakens my ear" (Isa. 50:4). Our ears represent ourselves. And when our ears are awakened to God, it means that we have become fully alert and ready to receive.

This emphasis on hearing God was distinctive to Judaism. Other religions contemporary to Israel emphasized *seeing* their gods. The worshipers of these religions wanted to have some kind of *vision*. And so they produced many idols and images.

But while they focused on seeing their gods, very often what was missing in those ancient religions was a message. A worshiper would go through the rituals that prepared him for his vision. But then he would leave his worship and go back to daily life with no message, no guidance and no inner change. The sacred moment for him was having a vision, not receiving a message or knowing where to go and how to live.

In contrast, Israel's God had a message to be heard, pondered and incorporated into life. And so, in the Jewish religion, there were no idols, images or pictures. Instead there was a message. And great care was given to duplicate, distribute and preserve that message.

As *seeing* faded into the background, *hearing* became more important, a fact repeatedly reflected in the prophets:

- Hear the word of the LORD (Isa. 1:10).
- Rise up and listen...hear what I have to say! (Isa. 32:9).
- Give ear and come to me; hear me, that your soul may live (Isa. 55:3).
- Hear and pay attention, do not be arrogant, for the LORD has spoken (Jer. 13:15).
- Hear the word of the LORD! (Ezek. 13:2).
- Now then, hear the word of the LORD (Amos 7:16).
- Listen to what the LORD says (Mic. 6:1).

Furthermore, everything and everyone is asked to "hear." The heavens (Isa. 1:2), earth (Isa. 1:2), scoffers (Isa. 28:14), nations (Jer. 31:10), exiles (Jer. 29:20), the house of Jacob (Jer. 2:4), the house of Israel (Jer. 10:1), the kings of Judah (Jer. 19:3), and Jerusalem (Jer. 19:3)—all must give God a hearing.

It is against this background that we can understand the heavy concentration of discernment words in Mark 4 (emphasis added):

- He taught them many things by parables, and in his teaching said: "*Listen!*" (4:2).
- He who has ears to *hear*, let him *hear* (4:9).
- They may be ever seeing but never perceiving, and ever *hearing* but never understanding (4:12).
- As soon as they *hear* it, Satan comes and takes away the word (4:15).
- Others...*hear* the word and at once receive it with joy. But since they have no root, they last only a short time (4:16,17).
- others...*hear* the word; but the worries of this life, the

deceitfulness of wealth and the desires for other things come in and choke the word (4:18,19).

- Others...*hear* the word, accept it, and produce a crop (4:20).
- If anyone has ears to *hear*, let him *hear* (4:23).
- Consider carefully what you *hear* (4:24).

Unquestionably, agriculture was the best possible metaphor that Jesus could have chosen to describe the process of hearing God. The agricultural stories picture God penetrating deep into the soil of our lives, putting down roots and growing. The smallest seed becomes the largest plant (4:31,32), and the good soil is fruitful (4:20) because we hear His message.

Of course, it is true that some hearing is independent of our will. We can't always choose the words that come our way each day. But according to Jesus, no sound has traveled its full course until it has reached the heart. In fact, in the New Testament, the ear is sometimes synonymous with the heart.

And so, some resist God with "uncircumcised hearts and ears" (Acts 7:51), while others respond to God's message with open hearts (see Acts 16:14). We see then why Jesus was so distressed with hearts that were "stubborn" (Mark 3:5), "far from" Him (Mark 7:6) or "hardened" (Mark 8:17). They wouldn't hear. The same message came to each ear, but a different priority was within each soul.

Consider the home of a small child, filled with sounds of every sort—stammering speech, broken syllables, faint resemblances of words. To the stranger, these sounds have little value. But to the mother, they are full of meaning. To her they are clear and she never tires of them. She doesn't hear them with a fleshly ear, but with a mother's heart. She is in tune with her child at the deepest level. This level of hearing symbolizes the open, responsive Christian who sincerely wants to hear God's message.

The parable of the soils is a parable of hearing. It teaches that we hear God with all we have made of ourselves. We hear Him with every sin that we cling to. We hear Him with our worries, ambitions and desires. We can't check them at the door; they come with us to meet the message of God as it

---

We hear Him with every sin that we cling to...with our worries, ambitions and desires....And we respond to God with welcome or defiance—it all depends on what we bring to the hearing.

---

is read or spoken. And we respond to God with welcome or defiance—it all depends on what we bring to the hearing.

Fred Craddock of Emory University says, "Listening is a quality of your character."[2] To want food requires hunger. To understand moral issues requires a certain morality. To discuss questions of conscience requires a conscience. To look at ethical concerns requires ethics. Jesus is insisting that, if we are to listen to Him, we must possess character. And so consider His plan for building character. At the end of the parable He gave these guidelines for hearing (Mark 4:20; Luke 8:15):

HEAR THE WORD

We must give the Word of God access to our hearts. Too many Christians view Scripture as raw information, and they go to it to get data or facts. Since their approach is analytic, they dissect the Word of God. They ignore His arrangement as they rearrange the dissected pieces of His Word into columns of information.

But Scripture is not just information to be arranged according to Aristotelian logic. God inspired men to write a story. And that's what Scripture is. It's a story. It's the story of men and women. It's the story of Jesus. It's the story of God. So, to really hear Jesus is to hear, understand and appreciate His story.

RETAIN THE WORD

Once the Word of God touches our hearts and we begin to appreciate its story, we must then be willing to obey its truth. We must ask questions like: What changes will this truth make in my life? How will it effect my relationships, my values and my purpose in life?

It is challenging to discover that in the New Testament, the Greek words for "obey" (*hypakouo*) and for "hear" (*akouo*) share the same root. Because "obey" is derived from "hear" is why "faith" has always been connected to "hearing." "Faith comes from hearing the message" (Rom. 10:17).

Obedience sharpens our ability to hear and understand. The more we respond to God's story, the clearer it becomes. This is how we retain what we have heard. This is how faith grows stronger. Obedience drives the hearing process deeper into our hearts.

PERSEVERE WITH THE WORD

Just as soon as we make plans to retain what we hear, Satan makes plans to uproot what God is growing in our lives. So we must persevere. We must identify the areas in which we are most vulnerable. Worry, wealth and desires are among the tactics Satan can use to "choke the word" (Mark 4:19). Not using what we have been given (see Mark 4:24) is another. But we have all done battle with Satan. We know where he usually strikes and we know our weaknesses. But will we persevere?

The more we respond to God's story, the clearer it becomes.....This is how faith grows stronger. Obedience drives the hearing process deeper into our hearts.

PRODUCE FROM THE WORD

An incredible power to produce resides in the seed of God's Word. This is the point of Jesus' parable of the growing seed:

> A man scatters seed on the ground. Night and day, whether he sleeps or gets up, the seed sprouts and grows, though he does not know how. All by itself the soil produces grain—first the stalk, then the head, then the full kernel in the head. As soon as the grain is ripe, he puts the sickle to it, because the harvest has come (Mark 4:26-28).

Our task is to hear, retain and persevere. God's is to produce. Paul wrote:

> I planted the seed, Apollos watered it, but God made it grow....We are God's fellow workers (1 Cor. 3:6,9).

We participate with God in the production, but "neither

he who plants nor he who waters is anything, but only God, who makes things grow" (1 Cor. 3:7). When we participate with God, His Spirit begins to produce power in our inner being (see Eph. 3:16), fruit in our attitudes (see Gal. 5:22) and unity in our relationships (see Eph. 2:14-18; Phil. 1:27).

But the process that leads to production begins with hearing, so be careful little ears what you hear.

FOR REFLECTION

1. What kind of things keep people from listening to Jesus?

2. What does Jesus mean by "he who has ears to hear, let him hear"?

3. What is the difference between looking at Scripture as information and as a story?

4. How is the emphasis on "hearing God" an emphasis distinctive to Judaism and Christianity?

5. What does it mean to open your heart to the message of God?

6. Why is it so tempting to turn religion into discussions about the fine points and debate over the insignificant?

7. What is your plan to retain what you hear from God?

8. Spend some time this week developing your listening. What did you learn about yourself, listening and others?

9. Why is listening hard work?

10. What are your areas of perseverance? Where does Satan usually attack you?

Notes
1. Public domain.
2. Fred B. Craddock, *Overhearing the Gospel* (Nashville: Abingdon, 1978), p. 36.

4
Crowd Me

Charles Dickens' *Pickwick Papers* pictures the power of a crowd:

> "It's always best on these occasions to do what the mob [does]."
> "But suppose there are two mobs?" suggested Mr. Snodgrass.
> "Shout with the largest," replied Mr. Pickwick.[1]

Whether it's a pep rally, a revival or a lynch mob, the morality of an individual can easily be diluted by a crowd. Sociologist Gustave Le Bon, in his classic, *The Crowd*, describes how a crowd can manipulate an individual:

> Isolated, he may be a cultivated individual; in a crowd, he is a barbarian....An individual in a crowd is a grain of sand amid other grains of sand, which the wind stirs up at will.[2]

The term "crowd" appears almost exclusively in the Gospels. Jesus constantly encountered groups of people. He taught them in synagogues, by the lakeside or in open fields. Often, He was feeding them. The 5,000 Jews. The 4,000 Gentiles.

Then, there were the healings. The blind, the lame, the diseased would crowd around Him. And it is in the crowd that we see the consistency of Jesus' character.

At first it seems odd that, while Jesus didn't seek crowds, they sought Him. His individual style of ministry attracted them. Yet He cared for individuals and gave them His time and attention. And so, early in the story, Jesus was constantly seeking individuals:

- Simon and Andrew (Mark 1:16)
- James and John (1:19)
- A possessed man (1:23)
- Simon's mother-in-law (1:30)
- A man with leprosy (1:40)
- A paralytic (2:3-5)
- A tax collector (2:14)
- A man with a shriveled hand (3:1)

But more and more, even as these individual incidents were occurring, the crowds were gathering:

- News about Jesus spread (1:28)
- The whole town gathered (1:33)
- Everyone looked for Jesus (1:37)
- People came from everywhere (1:45)
- There was no room left (2:2)
- A large crowd came to him (2:13)

Today's religious leaders play to the crowd. But that

wasn't Jesus' style. He issued no public notices. He wasn't concerned with visibility. He was concerned about people. And His persistent search for individual needs and hurts was matched by the swelling crowds:

Today's religious leaders play to the crowd. But that wasn't Jesus' style. He issued no public notices. He wasn't concerned with visibility. He was concerned about people.

Because of the crowd he told his disciples to have a small boat ready for him, to keep the people from crowding him. For he had healed many, so that those with diseases were pushing forward to touch him (Mark 3:9-10).

Usually, the crowd moved as a single unit with its own personality and temperament. Jesus had been successful with individuals—a guilty prostitute, an arrogant fisherman, even an ostracized tax collector. Yes, He had won the hearts of many individuals.

But crowds have no heart. They are unstable, volatile and constantly shifting. And with Jesus, they shifted through three stages.

STAGE ONE—JESUS WAS AMAZING

Early in the story, the crowds stood in awe of Jesus. He was incredible! They had never seen anything like Him. And so, they gathered around Him; amazed at His teaching, His compassion and His honesty.

- The people were amazed at his teaching (Mark 1:22).
- The people were all so amazed that they asked each other, "What is this? A new teaching—and with authority!" (Mark 1:27).
- He said to the paralytic, "I tell you, get up, take your mat and go home." He got up, took his mat and walked out in full view of them all. This amazed everyone and they praised God (Mark 2:10-12).
- And all the people were amazed (Mark 5:20).
- [She] stood up and walked around....At this they were completely astonished (Mark 5:42).

STAGE TWO—JESUS WAS USEFUL

After a while, the crowds grew accustomed to Jesus. His service was expected. For some, the awesome edge had begun to wear off. Jesus was becoming more useful than amazing:

- She came up behind him in the crowd and touched his cloak, because she thought, "If I just touch his clothes, I will be healed" (Mark 5:27-28).
- One of them, when he saw he was healed, came back, praising God in a loud voice....Jesus asked, "Were not all ten cleansed? Where are the other nine?" (Luke 17:15,17).

Many found practical uses for Jesus' compassion. Sometimes He was good for a free meal:

You are looking for me, not because you saw miraculous signs but because you ate the loaves and had your fill (John 6:26).

Others saw Jesus as a source of nationalistic power and change. A crowd of 5,000 wanted to use Him to lead their political uprising:

> Jesus, knowing that they intended to come and make him king by force, withdrew again into the hills by himself (John 6:15).

And then there were those who just wanted to see another trick:

> The Pharisees came....To test him, they asked him for a sign from heaven. He sighed deeply (Mark 8:11-12).

There were many crowds. And each was a conglomeration of shifting, selfish interests. To be used by the crowds must have been frustrating, even for Jesus. But manipulation of Him soon gave way to irritation with Him. Disillusioned with Jesus, the crowds shifted again.

STAGE THREE—JESUS WAS IN THE WAY

The seeds of hostility were planted early. Even while the crowds were still amazed with Jesus, the religious leaders were already planning His elimination.

> Then the Pharisees went out and began to plot with the Herodians how they might kill Jesus (Mark 3:6).

This conspiracy to do away with Him was no surprise to Jesus. The religious leaders had manipulated the crowds for years. Jesus knew how it would end:

> The chief priests stirred up the crowd to have Pilate release Barabbas instead.

"What shall I do, then, with the one you call the king of the Jews?" Pilate asked them.
"Crucify him!" they shouted (Mark 15:11-13).

Why the crowds shifted from one stage to another is an interesting study. But more interesting—and impressive—is the fact that Jesus *did not* shift. At every stage, He remained the same.

Early on, when the crowds stood in awe of Him, He reacted with both compassion and honesty. Notice first His compassion:

- So he went to her, took her hand and helped her up (Mark 1:31).
- Jesus healed many who had various diseases (Mark 1:34).
- Filled with compassion, Jesus reached out his hand and touched the man (Mark 1:41).
- Those with diseases were pushing forward to touch him (Mark 3:10).

The misery around Jesus ignited His compassion, resulting in a ministry of healing. How impressive to see someone respond to suffering rather than ignore it. But equally impressive was His honesty:

- He taught them as one who had authority (Mark 1:22).
- It is not the healthy who need a doctor, but the sick (Mark 2:17).
- No one pours new wine into old wineskins (Mark 2:22).
- Whoever does God's will is my brother and sister and mother (Mark 3:35).

- He who has ears to hear, let him hear (Mark 4:9).
- Consider carefully what you hear (Mark 4:24).

Jesus was always honest. He confronted people with their need for change. He challenged them to live a holy life. And His compassion gave credibility to his straightforward message.

However stage one didn't last very long. When the crowds shifted to stage two, Jesus didn't shift. He still gave compassion and honesty.

When the 5,000 put political pressure on Him (Mark 6:30-44; John 6:15), it made Him angry. How would you have felt? What happens to your compassion when you're angry?

Jesus *was* angry, but the 5,000 were hungry. And so with ongoing compassion, Jesus fed them.

> Taking the five loaves and the two fish and looking up to heaven, he gave thanks and broke the loaves. Then he gave them to his disciples to set before the people. He also divided the two fish among them all. They all ate and were satisfied (Mark 6:41-42).

Additionally, Jesus maintained His honest message. He not only fed the 5,000, He also taught them. And His teaching was forceful:

- You are looking for me, not because you saw miraculous signs but because you ate the loaves and had your fill. Do not work for food that spoils, but for food that endures to eternal life (John 6:26-27).
- "This is a hard teaching. Who can accept it?"...Many of his disciples turned back and no longer followed him (John 6:60,66).

When the crowds shifted the third time, Jesus must have found it especially difficult to maintain His compassion. For the crowd had begun to pull away those closest to Him:

> Judas, one of the Twelve, appeared. With him was a crowd (Mark 14:43).

The atmosphere was thick with betrayal. Peter reacted with violence and then cowardice (see Mark 14:47,50). But with characteristic compassion, Jesus healed the man Peter had wounded (see Luke 22:51). In spite of the betrayal and violence, Jesus was still serving; He actually healed the one who had come to arrest Him. And He gave them not only compassion, but also honesty:

> "Am I leading a rebellion," said Jesus...."Every day I was with you, teaching in the temple courts, and you did not arrest me" (Mark 14:48,49).

Even at the end of His life, when the cry, "Crucify him," went up, Jesus consistently offered compassion and honesty. He said things like:

- Forgive them, for they do not know what they are doing (Luke 23:34).
- Today you will be with me in paradise (Luke 23:43).

Jesus' encounters with crowds present Christians today with important lessons. Consider these:

IN PERSONAL FAITH—DON'T COMPROMISE YOUR VALUES

No crowd could compromise Jesus' values. But what *size* crowd defeats yours? What *kind* of crowd upsets your faith?

Have you found yourself doing things in a crowd that you would never do alone?

In Ministry—Seek the Individual

Have you ever tried to listen to a crowd? What do you hear? Do you hear the rumble and roar of the crowd—or do you hear the individuals in the crowd?

Have you ever tried to listen to a crowd? Do you hear the rumble and roar of the crowd—or do you hear the individuals?... Jesus heard the individuals.

Jesus heard the individuals. He heard their hunger, their distress, their moods and their fears. He didn't seek crowds; He sought individuals.

In Relationships—Refuse a Conglomerate Religion

The values of a crowd are formed by compromise. Everyone gives in to everyone else until a conglomerate conviction is formed. It is significant that, in the New Testament, the Church is not called a "crowd." Why? Because it is not a conglomerate religion.

The Church is called a "Body" because each individual receives his or her conviction from a single source, Jesus Christ, the Head of that Body. True, we stand as individuals before our Lord, but we also stand with each other as members of one Body (see 1 Cor. 12:12-13).

FOR REFLECTION

1. Why did Mark include encounters between Jesus and crowds?

2. Differentiate between a crowd and the Church.

3. Describe a crowd mentality.

4. Why did crowds always gather around Jesus?

5. What was Jesus' impact on the crowds?

6. Why do the moods of crowds shift so easily?

7. What are some of the demands made by crowds?

8. Why did the crowds so easily leave Jesus?

9. What basic lessons on discipleship did Jesus teach the crowds?

10. Give examples from your own life of how your faith has been tested by your peer group.

5

Interrupt Me

How do you handle interruptions?

Someone interrupts your conversation. Or the telephone rings at 2:00 in the morning. Or just as your carefully prepared plans are beginning to hit full stride, an unexpected problem changes everything.

Let's face it, we don't like interruptions, whether they are phone calls, flat tires, slow traffic or unplanned changes. We don't like the interruption. We don't like the intrusion. And we don't like the surprises. We like things to go on schedule.

Actually, we shouldn't be surprised at our own impatience. For impatience is the price that all time-worshipers must pay. If Americans are not the most time-conscious of all people, why then does American English contain more references to the concept of time than any spoken language currently in use?

In business we say, "Time is money." And so we carry personal beepers and pocket calendars. We attend time management seminars and purchase cellular phones for our cars.

The last thing we want or need are interruptions. Our time is just too valuable.

But are interruptions a modern phenomenon? Is busyness really distinctive to our own time? Certainly not! In fact, one of the distinctive messages of the Gospel of Mark is the incredible pace of Jesus. Underscoring this fact is Mark's frequent use of the word "immediately" while narrating events in Jesus' life:

- *Immediately* he saw the heavens opened and the Spirit descending (1:10, *RSV*).
- The Spirit *immediately* drove him out into the wilderness (1:12, *RSV*).
- And *immediately* they left their nets and followed him (1:18, *RSV*).
- And *immediately* he called them (1:20, *RSV*).
- *Immediately* on the sabbath he entered the synagogue and taught (1:21, *RSV*).
- And *immediately* there was in their synagogue a man with an unclean spirit (1:23, *RSV*).
- And *immediately* his fame spread abroad throughout all the region round about Galilee (1:28, *KJV*).
- And *immediately* he left the synagogue (1:29, *RSV*).
- *Immediately* they told him of her. And he came and took her by the hand (1:30,31, *RSV*).

This word "immediately" occurs 11 times in the combined Gospels of Matthew, Luke and John. But in Mark, the shortest of the Gospels, it occurs 42 times! Mark is telling us that Jesus was busy! He was pressed by demands on His time and schedule.

In these seven stories of interruption, put yourself in Jesus' place and see how close your reactions are to those recorded here:

MARK 1:35-37—LOOKING FOR SOLITUDE

You have made plans to be alone. You want to be free of interruptions, because you need to pray. So you get up early in the morning, long before the time anyone will need you. And you not only find a *time* to pray, but you also find a *place*, "a solitary place" (v. 35).

But, somewhere in the middle of your prayer, you feel the hand of interruption on your shoulder. Lifting your head, you see your disciples, and they say to you, "Everyone is looking for you" (v. 37).

Inside you respond, "I know! That's why I got up so early. I needed to be away from everybody." But your thoughts remain inside. You feel them, but you don't say them.

2:1-12—TEACHING A LESSON

You're teaching in Capernaum. A large crowd has gathered to hear you. You have something important to say to this crowd. Many of the people have traveled long distances to be here. Clearly you have everyone's attention. But just as you reach a turning point in your message, a loud, messy interruption occurs—the roof just over your head caves in.

3:20-21—TRYING TO EAT

It's been a very busy time for you. Looking back, you remember the man whose hand was deformed. You felt his pain. Not long after that, a group of Pharisees came looking for a reason to accuse you. Their stubbornness greatly distressed you.

Then there were the crowds. They were always there to watch you or to ask questions. And in the middle of all this activity, you've been trying to find time to eat. But the interruptions won't allow it. Finally your family hears that you're

not eating. They come to put a stop to this madness themselves.

4:35-41—SEEKING SOME REST

You've been so busy lately that you're exhausted. People are
everywhere. So much has happened. And so many demands
have been made upon you.

Standing by the lake, you tell your disciples, "Let us go
over to the other side" (v. 35).

As you leave the crowd, you collapse on a cushion in the
boat and fall asleep. But just as you're beginning to regain
some much needed strength and rest, the hand of interruption shakes you awake. As you open your eyes, the first
words you hear are, "Teacher, don't you care?" (v. 38).

Suddenly, everything inside of you wants to scream,
"What do you mean, 'Don't you care'? What do you think
I've been doing for the past week? I'm caring for people all
the time!"

But again, you control your emotion; you don't say all
that you feel. Instead, you deal with their fear, teach them
about faith—and go on.

5:21-34—PREPARING TO SPEAK

You have just returned by boat from an exhausting encounter
with a demoniac from the Gerasene region. Again, a large
crowd has gathered to hear you. It's a tremendous opportunity to speak to people about God.

But just as your foot touches the shoreline, your plans are
interrupted by a plea for help. Jairus, a synagogue leader,
says, "My little daughter is dying. Please come" (v. 23).

So you cancel your plans and prepare to go with Jairus.
But again, just as you are leaving with him, his interruption

is, in turn, interrupted by a desperate woman also reaching out to you for help.

6:30-34—PLANNING WITH FRIENDS

The crowds are growing. The word is spreading all over Galilee. Everybody wants you. No one seems to understand that you can be in only one place at a time.

You plan some time to be alone with the Twelve. But so

Aggressive, almost pushy faith is the kind that Jesus...praises in parables.... Today we have the same choice that Jesus had. We can focus on the outside...or we can look deeper and see persistence and faith.

---

many people recognize you and the needs are so great, that you delay your plans with the Twelve. Instead, you go with the interruption. You feed and teach the crowd.

15:29-32—DYING IN AGONY

You're dying. Words cannot express the pain you are experiencing. It's difficult to breathe. You're losing blood.

But even your pain is interrupted. First, there is the desperate plea of a thief. And, in spite of your own situation, you help him. But there are also the taunts: "Come down from the cross and save yourself!" (v. 30) "He saved others,...but he can't save himself!" (v. 31).

Even at the end of your life you have no time to yourself.

You are not dying at home with your family. Instead, you are made to die a criminal's death in a public spectacle. No one is holding your hand or whispering words of affection. Even the process of dying is interrupted and debased with scattered abuse and insults.

These situations from the life of Jesus challenge busy Christians today. How do *we* handle interruptions? How do *we* feel when somebody interrupts our speech, our meals or our sleep? How would *we* react if someone interrupted our worship service—even if that person left the roof intact?

These seven stories of interruption are for business executives who are pressured by deadlines, for students who are pressed by the demands of school, and for parents who are caught between career and children. All of us should consider these lessons from Jesus' interruptions:

JESUS RECEIVED TWO KINDS OF INTERRUPTIONS— CRITICISM AND FAITH

Jesus was interrupted by critics: Pharisees, Sadducees, scribes—they all interrupted him. But Jesus gave limited or no time to the critic who came with a trick or a trap.

But the woman who interrupted the interruption by Jairus (Mark 5:28) was different. True, her touch was *anonymous*—and some would judge this to be the worst kind of interruption. But she had wanted to steal some help and when she was discovered, she fell at Jesus' feet in fear.

Certainly her touch was an interruption, but it was an *expectant* interruption. Her suffering was as old as Jairus' daughter—12 years. Yet despite her pain she still had hope.

She was looking for something. And her *impersonal* interruption brought *personal* attention. Jesus saw, in her interruption, a struggling faith that He wanted to develop. He saw her, not just as an interruption, but as an interruption of faith.

JESUS LOOKED PAST OUTWARD INTERRUPTION TO INWARD MOTIVATION

In the story of the paralytic (Mark 2:1-12), Jesus saw past the outward interruption of the four friends to their *eagerness* to get their friend to Jesus. He saw the *courage* that enabled them to do something as unconventional as digging through a roof. He saw a *persistence* that refused to be stopped by the crowds. And behind these characteristics, He saw *faith* breaking through the layers of brushwood and mud (v. 5).

This aggressive, almost pushy faith is the kind that Jesus later praises in parables (Luke 11:5-8; 18:1-8). Today we have the same choice that Jesus had. We can focus on the outside, on the irritation that the interruption brings. Or we can look deeper and see eagerness, courage, persistence and faith.

JESUS SAW INTERRUPTIONS AS OPPORTUNITIES

Looking only at the obvious, we can very easily assume that the interruptions Jesus experienced were caused by outside forces—the crowds, the woman, Jairus, the paralytic, the lepers. We naturally suppose they caused the interruptions.

But isn't it true that Jesus dealt with people in a way that let them know they could interrupt Him? His style of ministry invited interruption. Why? Because He saw the interruptions as His work rather than as hindrances to His work.

He was approachable. He was easy to talk to. In short, He was easy to interrupt.

JESUS DESCRIBED THE LAST INTERRUPTION

In Mark 13:32-35 Jesus describes the last interruption mankind will ever experience. This event is sometimes called "The Second Coming."

No one knows about that day or hour, not even the angels in heaven, nor the Son, but only the Father. Be on guard! Be alert! You do not know when that time will come.

It's like a man going away: He leaves his house in charge of his servants, each with his assigned task, and tells the one at the door to keep watch.

Therefore keep watch because you do not know when the owner of the house will come back—whether in the evening, or at midnight, or when the rooster crows, or at dawn.

Our last interruption will come from the hand of God. And our readiness for this last interruption will depend on how we have handled all of the other interruptions in our Christian life. Did we simply react with irritation? Or did we take the time to look past the interruptions to the deeper motivations?

Did we make it clear that we didn't want to be bothered? Or did we see and use the opportunity to serve? Were people more important to us than time?

Jesus says:

If he comes suddenly, do not let him find you sleeping. What I say to you, I say to everyone: Watch! (13:36-37).

FOR REFLECTION

1. How do you feel when someone interrupts you?

2. How do Americans perceive "time"?

3. Retell three of the stories where people interrupted Jesus.

4. Which interruption in Mark speaks most to your life?

5. Since Jesus has so many important things to do and say, why does He allow people to interrupt Him?

6. How does Mark describe the pace of Jesus?

7. Describe the two kinds of interruptions to Jesus?

8. Who really caused the interruptions in the life of Jesus?

9. What are some ways you can improve your attitude toward people who interrupt you?

10. How do we prepare for the last interruption of life?

6
Touch Me

The headline read, "TOUCHING REQUIRED AT NEW AREA MUSE-UM." Recognizing the teaching power of touch, this children's museum constructed a series of hands-on exhibits. Inviting visitors to touch the exhibits was quite a break from the past when museums normally posted signs which read "Keep Off" and "Do Not Touch."

What message do you receive when someone refuses to shake hands with you? Do you feel wanted or accepted? No! You feel rejected and embarrassed. Perhaps you even feel angry. If you offer your touch and it is refused, it means *you* are refused.

A husband pulls away. A wife says, "Don't touch me." But neither the husband nor the wife are refusing touch as much as they are refusing what touch stands for—their relationship.

Jesus' touch symbolized God's relationship with the human race. Jesus understood the power of touch and made it central in His ministry, as these incidents in the Gospel of Mark indicate (emphasis added):

- Simon's mother-in-law was in bed with a fever, and they told Jesus about her. So he went to her, *took her hand* and helped her up. The fever left her and she began to wait on them (Mark 1:30-31).
- Filled with compassion, Jesus reached out his hand and *touched* the man. "I am willing," he said. "Be clean!" (1:41).
- He had healed many, so that those with diseases were pushing forward to *touch* him (3:10).
- A large crowd followed and *pressed around him.* And a woman was there who had been subject to bleeding for twelve years....she came up behind him in the crowd and *touched* his cloak, because she thought, "If I just *touch* his clothes, I will be healed" (5:24,25,27,28).
- He *took her by the hand* and said to her, "*Talitha koum!*" (5:41).
- They begged him to let them *touch* even the edge of his cloak, and all who *touched* him were healed (6:56).
- They begged him to *place his hand on the man....Jesus put his fingers into the man's ears.* Then he spit and *touched* the man's tongue (7:32-33).
- He *took the blind man by the hand*...and *put his hands on him,* Once more Jesus *put his hands on the man's eyes.* Then his eyes were opened, his sight was restored, and he saw everything clearly (8:23,25).
- The boy looked so much like a corpse that many said, "He's dead." But Jesus *took him by the hand* and lifted him to his feet, and he stood up (9:26-27).

Jesus touched the "untouchable"—the diseased, the guilty, the outcasts and the dead. To use the language of the *King James Version* (emphasis added):

> We have not an high priest which cannot be *touched* with the feeling of our infirmities (Heb.4:15).

Jesus even taught that the Kingdom was reserved for those who touched:

> For I was hungry and you gave me something
>   to eat,
> I was thirsty and you gave me something to
>   drink,
> I was a stranger and you invited me in,
> I needed clothes and you clothed me,
> I was sick and you looked after me,
> I was in prison and you came to visit me
> (Matt. 25:35-36).

Jesus conducted a high-touch ministry which stood in stark contrast to the no-touch attitudes and actions of the world around Him:

- When the teachers of the law who were Pharisees saw him eating with the "sinners" and tax collectors, they asked his disciples: "Why does he eat with tax collectors and 'sinners'?" (Mark 2:16).
- People were bringing little children to Jesus to have him touch them, but the disciples rebuked them (Mark 10:13).
- A blind man, Bartimaeus...was sitting by the roadside begging. When he heard that it was Jesus of Nazareth, he began to shout, "Jesus, Son of David, have mercy on me!" Many rebuked him and told him to be quiet (Mark 10:46-48).
- The Samaritan woman said to him, "You are a Jew and I am a Samaritan woman. How can you ask me for a drink?" (For Jews do not associate with Samaritans.) (John 4:9).
- When the Pharisee who had invited him saw this, he said to himself, "If this man were a prophet, he

would know who is touching him and what kind of woman she is—that she is a sinner" (Luke 7:39).

- A man was going down from Jerusalem to Jericho, when he fell into the hands of robbers. They stripped him of his clothes, beat him and went away, leaving him half dead. A priest happened to be going down the same road, and when he saw the man, he passed by on the other side (Luke 10:30-31).

The world in which Jesus lived was fragmented. Huge walls separated the various classes of people. The distance was measured in units of resentment, alienation and pride. No one crossed over or even reached over those walls.

But Jesus leaped over them by extending His hand to touch. He believed in the tremendous power of touch. It was a power on three levels:

The Physical Power of Touch

Today we speak of "rubbing" people the wrong way or of "stroking" them the right way. We want to get in "touch" with someone, or we describe someone as having a "soft touch." Some people are "touchy" while others are "thick-skinned."

Touch is a deeply felt experience. It is the parent of our eyes, ears, nose and mouth. Dr. Ashley Montagu wrote: "The sense of touch, 'the mother of the senses,' is the earliest to develop in the human embryo."[1]

When we say someone is "tactful" we usually mean that person is emotionally sensitive and good with his or her words. Certainly Jesus was emotionally sensitive with His words. But the literal meaning of "tact" is "to touch." It is hands-on; it is physical. And in this sense Jesus was tactful in a tactless world—He physically touched people.

Today we wash before and brush after every meal. We can't stand the smell of our own body odor after an afternoon of working in the yard. But Jesus managed the sight, the stench and even the touch of first-century disease.

The world in which Jesus lived was fragmented. Huge walls separated the various classes of people. Jesus leaped over those walls by extending His hand to touch.

Some of those He touched had not been touched in years: Lepers with decaying skin. Ears clogged with years of deafness. Eyes caked with disease. Running sores. Bleeding wounds. Deformed limbs.

Jesus touched them all. And His touch soothed, healed and revealed His desire to help. In Jesus' touch was physical power. But His touch went even deeper.

THE EMOTIONAL POWER OF TOUCH

Psychologist James Lynch has spent hours in coronary care units watching people visit loved ones who are faced with the possibility of sudden death. In his book, *The Broken Heart*, he observed:

> I have been struck by the way most people finally say good-bye....Just before leaving, they will stop speaking and silently hold the patient's hand or

touch his body or even stand at the foot of the bed and hold the patient's foot....

More often than not, the final good-bye does not involve words, almost as if words alone were insufficient to communicate their true feelings. The most simple and direct type of human communication does not need words.[2]

Greg Risberg, clinical social worker and lecturer at the Northwestern University Medical School, told the story of a young man he met in Chicago. The man was single and completely alone in the big city:

This man would check the newspaper for obituaries, and when he found a funeral near his home, he would get all dressed up and go visit the family just so he could be touched....He felt crummy about it, but he needed to be touched so bad.[3]

Jesus knew that beneath the physical wounds were deeper emotional wounds. So in spite of health hazards and public opinion, He reached out to a person's deepest fears and anxieties. And He made them bearable and manageable by sharing them.

Carry each other's burdens, and in this way you will fulfill the law of Christ (Gal. 6:2).

We all have thoughts and emotions so deep and personal that words alone cannot bear their weight. They cry out for touch. And in our sterile, technological culture we need the closeness and intimacy of touch more than ever. We need to share ourselves with each other as surely as we need to breathe. We need to be like Jesus.

Jesus demonstrated that touch has physical and emotional power. But so have many other compassionate people. The distinctiveness of Jesus' touch is found in a larger, more fundamental reality—one which includes and gives deeper meaning to both the physical and emotional power of touch.

We all have thoughts and emotions so deep... that words alone cannot bear their weight. They cry out for touch. In our sterile, culture we need the...intimacy of touch more than ever. We need to be like Jesus.

THE SPIRITUAL POWER OF TOUCH

Our physical and emotional wounds are overshadowed by our spiritual plight. At least Jesus thought so. His first words to the paralytic were not "take your mat and walk," but "Son, your *sins* are forgiven" (Mark 2:5,10, emphasis added).

Unfortunately most are not aware of the deeper origin of their pain. And while they welcome physical and emotional healing, their ultimate need remains untouched. They need His spiritual touch.

When we consider the spiritual power of touch, as we learn it from Jesus, it helps to think of it in these six terms:

Presence
Jesus stands with us and touches and experiences our deepest pain, our heaviest burden—our guilt. He is called "Immanuel" which means "God with us" (Matt. 1:23). He

truly is "an ever *present* help in time of trouble" (Ps. 46:1, emphasis added).

Identification
Them and us. Rich and poor. Majority and minority. The walls separating these and other groups are huge, and the gap is growing wider. But no gap can compare to the one separating human and divine, finite and infinite, sinful and sinless, God and the human race. Yet Jesus bridged that chasm by becoming one of us.

Affirmation
The word "dignity" comes from the Latin *dignus* which literally means "worthy." The spiritual touch of Jesus was a declaration that the human race has great worth. This truth is what fueled His ministry—He thinks we are worth it!

Security
Just as children call out in the night, asking for a reassuring touch, so do the blind, the lame, the forgotten and the guilty. They ask, "Is there any security? Is there any stability? Is there anything we can depend on?"

The touch of Jesus says, "Yes. You can depend on me."

Affection
Touching is an almost universally accepted gesture of affection and comfort. In a world of guilt and hopelessness the touch of Jesus brings forgiveness, meaning, comfort and hope. Yes, He cares about the guilty.

God touched us once when He formed us from dust and gave us His image (see Gen 1:26,27; 2:7). In Jesus, He touches us again. And the one event in particular where the physical, emotional and spiritual all converge is the cross of Jesus.

THE CROSS WAS A PHYSICAL EVENT

They...twisted together a crown of thorns and set it on him....They struck him on the head with a staff and spit on him....They led him out to crucify him....They crucified him (Mark 15:17,19,20,24).

THE CROSS WAS AN EMOTIONAL EVENT

He began to be deeply distressed and troubled. "My soul is overwhelmed with sorrow to the point of death" (Mark 14:33-34).

THE CROSS WAS A SPIRITUAL EVENT

And at the ninth hour Jesus cried out in a loud voice, *"Eloi, Eloi, lama sabachthani?"*—which means, "My God, my God, why have you forsaken me?" (Mark 15:33).

The cross is the place where Jesus extends His hand to touch us on every level. It is the place where we come into full contact with Jesus. In the cross we are "with him" (emphasis added):

- *"with him*...in his death" (Rom. 6:5).
- *"with him* in his resurrection" (6:5).
- "crucified *with him"*(6:6).
- "buried *with him"* (6:4).
- "live *with him"* (6:8).

FOR REFLECTION

1. What is the physical power of touch?

2. What is the spiritual power of touch?

3. In what sense is God a touching God?

4. Why do human beings need to be needed in order to be healthy and mature?

5. What is the relationship between love and touching?

6. What is the emotional power of touch?

7. Why is there not more touching in the Church?

8. What can a church do to encourage appropriate "touching" among its members?

9. How has our culture affected the Church's understanding of touching?

10. What practical steps can families take to encourage affection and touching?

Notes

1. Dr. Ashley Montagu, *Touching: The Human Significance of Skin* (New York: Columbia University Press, 1971), p. 1.
2. James J. Lynch, *The Broken Heart: The Medical Consequences of Loneliness* (New York: Basic Books, Inc. Publishers, 1938), pp. 126-27.
3. Laurie Glenn, "Touch Someone," Springfield *Leader & Press*, March 14, 1985.

7
Fear Me

Consider three stories:

The *first* consists of accounts of teenage violence which has become so savage that it has spawned a new word— "wilding."[1]

- In New York City's Central Park, a woman jogger was brutally beaten and raped by teenagers, all between 14 and 17 years old. When asked why they had attacked her, one of the teenage suspects replied, "It was fun."
- In Brooklyn, New York, three teenagers attempted to set fire to a homeless couple. After failing with rubbing alcohol, they finally succeeded with gasoline.
- In rural Missouri, three teenagers killed a friend— out of curiosity! Again, the stated reason for this violence was, "Because it's fun."

The "wilding" story is a story of evil.

The *second* story is about a child abuse hot line and a full-page ad that said, "Nearly one million children would be glad to call the number below. Except they are busy being beaten, neglected, and molested."[2]

The ad reminds us that child abuse is up 80 percent in one decade. In this single statistic we learn where the teenage "wilding" story had its beginnings. It was born out of abuse and neglect where the violated grow up to be violent.

Consider the plight of children in our country. Each day:

- 72 babies die before one month of life.
- 110 babies die before their first birthday.
- 8 children die from gunshot wounds.
- 988 children are abused.
- 3,288 children run away from home.
- 49,322 children are in public juvenile-correctional facilities.
- 2,989 children see their parents divorced.
- 2,269 children are born illegitimately.[3]

This story also is a story of evil.

The *third* story is about two boys who grew up together. They were friends. They played together. They went to the same school. And both of them discovered evil at about the same time. But one learned to talk about it with interested parents, while the other hid it. They grew up with very different views of evil.

Today, one of them still copes with evil. He had early training and he learned to love good and to resist evil. He learned to confess evil when it occurred and to receive help.

The other young man never really coped with evil. Instead, he welcomed it. He learned to hide evil when it occurred in his life until he finally didn't care who knew. Evil always had an unobstructed channel in his life. It became entrenched and eventually destroyed him. The story of Jesus is a story of encounters. Most of the time we think of His encounters with people. But He also encountered evil.

In Mark's description, the term translated "evil" in the *New International Version* and "unclean" in the *King James Version* literally means "the opposite of good." Take a few moments to read the following stories of Jesus' encounter with evil:

- Jesus drives an evil spirit from a young man (1:23-26).
- In the evening Jesus drives out demons, drives out evil (1:32-34).
- Jesus states that His purpose is to preach and drive out demons (1:38-39).
- Whenever the evil spirits see Jesus they cry out in terror (3:11-12).
- Jesus helps a man possessed by a legion of evil demons (5:1-20).
- The Twelve are sent to preach, heal and drive out evil spirits (6:7-13).
- Jesus helps a woman whose daughter is possessed (7:24-30).
- Jesus drives an evil spirit out of a man's son (9:17-29).

First, notice that these clashes were filled with fear. The confrontation between good and evil always brought terror to the surface. Evil was always afraid when confronted by the Son of God. This truth is significant in the ministry of One who regularly said, "Don't be afraid."

Second, evil spirits always recognized Jesus. In fact, the stories reveal that they recognized Him long before anyone else did. In the first encounter, the evil spirit said, "I know who you are—the Holy One of God" (1:24). In the next occurrence, Jesus "would not let the demons speak because they knew who he was" (1:34). Evil recognized Jesus and cried out in terror.

Third, up to this point, evil always could be driven out. Every confrontation had the same ending—exorcism.

But as the Gospel of Mark turns the corner, the encounters with evil spirits begin to thin out.

- Three encounters in chapter 1.
- Three encounters in chapter 3.
- One encounter in chapter 5.
- One encounter in chapter 6.
- One encounter in chapter 7.
- One encounter in chapter 9.

The conflicts with evil spirits seemingly began to decrease as Jesus approached Jerusalem. Possibly, Mark is just reporting fewer instances. Yet Matthew, Luke and John also tell the story of Jesus in the same way.

When Jesus turned south to go to Jerusalem, His encounters with evil spirits diminished and then stopped. But notice that His fight with evil did not stop. Instead, it intensified. Jesus then faced an evil that was more entrenched.

In fact, the closer Jesus came to Jerusalem, the less He encountered evil that could be driven out. This evil had fully permeated life. He encountered no foaming mouths or twisted bodies there. The merger of evil and life had been successful.

What evil fits this description? This is the picture of the religious establishment that Jesus confronted more and more as He approached Jerusalem. Earlier, Jesus had dealt with children who wanted the evil out of their lives. And when the evil was cast out, it had left a widow's daughter (7:30) and a man's son (9:26-27) whole.

Even before these encounters, Jesus healed a man whose fight with evil was so great that when Jesus asked the name of the evil spirit which possessed him, He was given a number equal to that of an entire Roman army unit: "My name is Legion [Six Thousand]" (5:9). But this man wanted the evil out. And when Jesus sent it out, it left a new missionary (5:19-20).

But all that had been before. Now, as Jesus approached

Evil can and will become entrenched in our lives when we no longer resist. We eventually welcome evil and even begin to look for new forms.

Jerusalem and entered the city, He began to encounter an evil that was so entrenched and so blended with human life that He didn't even attempt to cast it out. Mark first mentioned this more deadly kind of evil when Jesus healed a man with a shriveled hand on the Sabbath (3:1-6).

Jesus sensed the evil in the Pharisees who "were looking for a reason to accuse" Him (3:2), and He confronted them. Their first reaction was silence. They were stubborn. The evil had so permeated their lives that they did not want to let go of it.

Their second reaction was to plot His murder (3:6). Evil was so ingrained in them that, while they criticized Jesus for *healing* on their holy day, they used that same day to plan a *killing.*

Later, Jesus battled with Pharisees and teachers of the law who traveled the distance from Jerusalem to Galilee to look for a reason to criticize (7:1-23). They found it—Jesus ate the wrong way.

Jesus again confronted the evil: "You have let go of the commands of God" (7:8). "You nullify the word of God" (7:13).

Yet though He exposed their evil as "unclean" (v. 20), He did not try to drive it out because they embraced it so tightly.

How different is the demoniac who ran to Jesus and fell on his knees, wanting the evil to be taken out. Or the mother who brought her little girl to Jesus and begged Him to take the evil out. Not so with these religious professionals. They accepted evil.

In fact, evil worked harmoniously with religious prestige and community recognition to manipulate crowds, to bring false accusations, to pay off traitors and to orchestrate the murder of the Son of God. This evil, though not as dramatic as that of the possession cases in earlier stories, was more entrenched, more at home and much more deadly.

We can learn much from Jesus' encounter with evil. Consider these lessons:

GOD CAN DRIVE EVIL FROM MY LIFE IF I WANT IT OUT

Jesus' brother wrote, "Submit yourselves, then, to God. Resist the devil, and he will flee from you" (Jas. 4:7). Evil was afraid of Jesus early in the story because it was resisted. It was not wanted.

But if I give evil a home in my life, even my religion will become twisted and deadly. God will not work in my life against my will. I must resist Satan and submit to God.

EVIL CAN BECOME ENTRENCHED

Yes, evil can and will become entrenched in our lives when we no longer resist. We eventually welcome evil and even begin to look for new forms. When evil becomes this established in a person's life, that person will begin to feel the fear that comes with it.

Early in the story of Jesus' encounters with evil, the demons cried out in fear. But later that fear was shared, becoming widespread. Herod was afraid of John (Mark 6:20). The priests feared Jesus (11:18). The teachers of the law feared the people (11:32). The religious establishment was

---

When evil finds a home, fear also finds a home. But when evil is resisted, the message, "Don't be afraid," begins to make sense. Decide to give the fear back to Satan by making evil homeless in your life.

---

afraid of the crowd (12:12).

When evil finds a home, fear also finds a home. But when evil is resisted, the message, "Don't be afraid," begins to make sense. Decide to give the fear back to Satan by making evil homeless in your life.

EVIL CAN BECOME ENTRENCHED IN RELIGION

Who resisted God? Who lied? Who killed Jesus?

It was the religious establishment. Being a religious person is no guarantee that evil will not infiltrate a person's life. Evil has a long history of harmonious cooperation with religion.

A minister once conducted a seminar in St. Louis for people who had been burned by religion. It served as a bridge to God. It provided a place to begin talking about God. But the minister didn't mention God during the entire three-night seminar.

After one of the evening sessions a couple came up to him and expressed their appreciation for what they had been learning. Then, with a puzzled look, they asked, "But do you really think you can have all of these good things without religion?"

The minister answered, "Yes, but not without God."

The couple looked surprised and said, "You are the first person we have ever heard distinguish between religion and God."

That night an important lesson was taught. One form of religion can love God and resist evil, while another kind of religion can plot the murder of the Son of God.

GOOD IS MORE POWERFUL THAN EVIL

C. S. Lewis, is the author of *The Screwtape Letters,* a revealing fiction about the correspondence between Screwtape, a senior devil, and his nephew, Wormwood, who is in tempter-training school. After writing the book, Lewis was asked if he really believed in the devil. He answered:

> Now if by the devil you mean a power opposite to God and like God, self-existent from all eternity, the answer is certainly No....God has no opposite....
>
> The proper question is whether I believe in devils. I do. That is to say, I believe in angels, and I believe that some of these, by the abuse of their free will, have become enemies to God and, as a corollary, to us....
>
> Devil is the opposite of angel only as Bad Man is the opposite of Good Man. Satan, the leader or dictator of devils, is the opposite, not of God, but of Michael.[4]

Satan is a fallen angel who can never match the power of God. God is infinitely more powerful than any evil. But as we have seen from these stories in Mark, God works through choice, confession and commitment. Evil may be powerful, but He who epitomized the greater power of good says, "Don't be afraid."

FOR REFLECTION

1. Tell an experience in which you felt deep fear.

2. Give two examples from Mark in which Jesus encountered evil.

3. What is there about evil spirits that you do not understand?

4. Why are demons and evil spirits so foreign to us?

5. Why does Mark set the encounters of Jesus with evil spirits at the *beginning* of his Gospel?

6. How does Jesus' clash with evil intensify as He approaches Jerusalem?

7. How does evil fight Jesus in Jerusalem?

8. How is the evil in Jerusalem less obvious and more dangerous than demons or evil spirits?

9. Who should fear Jesus? Why?

10. What kinds of evil are you facing in your own life and how can you overcome them?

Notes

1. "Some Reasons for 'Wilding,'" *Newsweek*, May 29, 1989, pp. 6-7.
2. *U.S. News & World Report*, April 2, 1990.
3. *U.S. News & World Report*, November 7, 1988.
4. C. S. Lewis, *The Joyful Christian: 127 Readings from C. S. Lewis* (New York: Macmillan Publishing Co., Inc., 1977), pp. 145-46.

8
Oppose Me

Popularly called "hardening of the arteries," arteriosclerosis is a well-known health hazard. Many suffer from it or know someone who does. But another condition exists that is just as common, though perhaps not as widely recognized—because it is not a medical condition.

This hazard is not a thickening of the walls of a person's arteries. Rather, it is an attitude condition, a hardening of a person's heart. We might call it "categoriosclerosis" or a "hardening of the categories."

This chronically resistant condition which occurs throughout society can prevent learning and often destroys relationships. It shows itself when a person holds to a viewpoint out of stubbornness rather than from reasoned study. And in religion, categoriosclerosis occurs when a person chooses tradition over the command of God.

When God entered human history as the man Jesus, He found a religious culture infected with severe hardening of the categories. The Gospel of Mark showed Jesus facing the political hopes of an oppressed Palestine, but His mission was not political. He spoke out against the social inequities of His day, but His mission was not social reform. He healed the sick, the lame and the blind, but His mission was neither physical nor medical.

The ministry of Jesus did touch many areas, but at its core, it was always essentially religious.

For example, in Mark 11, Jesus faced a politically tense situation. It was Passover time, the festival that memorialized Israel's political rescue from Egypt. And Passover always brought to mind God's ancient champion, Moses. So Jesus knew that the expectation of another champion was very high.

Yet though the atmosphere was filled with dangerous tension, it all ended quietly. No political explosion occurred. Why? What happened?

Notice that, after entering the city, Jesus turned the *political* parade into a *religious* statement. Instead of storming the Roman garrison or making political speeches about Roman tyranny, Jesus led a procession to the Temple. It is as if He were saying, "Yes, I am leading a rebellion, but not against Rome. I am against what is really wrong, and I find it in your Temple, in your religion."

Clearly, His mission was religious.

In Mark 2, four men brought a medical problem to Jesus—their paralytic friend. But, the first words from Jesus mouth were not "Take up your mat and walk," but "Son, your sins are forgiven" (v. 5).

In fact, the focus of this story is not the physical healing at all. Rather, the focus of the story is the faith of the paralytic contrasted with the hard-hearted religion exhibited by the teachers of the law.

All the various travels and experiences of Jesus clearly led to His eventual destination—Jerusalem. All four Gospels ultimately take the story to Jerusalem, the center of religion.

In actuality, the Gospel of Luke presents all the other facets of Jesus' ministry simply as pieces of this journey.

Because Jesus' mission was fundamentally religious, Luke takes great care to show a deliberate trek to the city:

- Moses and Elijah speak of Jesus' work in Jerusalem (9:30-31).
- Jesus resolutely set out for *Jerusalem* (9:51).
- He is headed for *Jerusalem* (9:53).
- He makes His way to *Jerusalem* (13:22).
- He predicts His death in *Jerusalem* (13:33).
- He is on His way to *Jerusalem* (17:11).
- He talks about what will happen in *Jerusalem* (18:31).
- He is near *Jerusalem* (19:11).
- He goes on ahead to *Jerusalem* (19:28).
- He approaches *Jerusalem* and weeps over it (19:41).

Of course, it would have been much easier for Jesus to have accepted the political mission of the 5,000 patriots (Mark 6:30-44), who came to make Him king by force (John 6:15). He would have made a great king. Or it would have been easier for Him to have stayed in Galilee to maintain a social reform program and medical mission.

But He resisted the temptation to be sidetracked. "Let us go somewhere else—to the nearby villages—so I can preach there also. That is why I have come" (Mark 1:38).

Jesus' determination put Him on a collision course with the religious establishment. Religion's categories had grown hard. Its leadership and direction had become a burden to the purposes of God. And so, conflict was unavoidable.

Christ the Controversialist, by John R. W. Stott is a study of the areas of conflict. He introduces the book in this way:

Jesus lived a stormy life. His teachings angered the

Establishment and brought him face to face with those who disagreed—Pharisees who were shocked at his lack of respect for their traditions, Sadducees who could not accept Jesus' view of the afterlife....[1]

True, Jesus' life was a stormy one. But notice in Mark how the storm of opposition had grown gradually:

- Jesus' authority was contrasted with the teachers of the law (Mark 1:21-22).
- Criticism of Him began—"Why does this fellow talk like that?" (2:1-12).
- The Pharisees criticized the company Jesus kept (2:15-17).
- Jesus was criticized for his lack of ritual fasting (2:18).
- The Pharisees criticized Jesus' disregard for their traditions (2:23-28).
- The opposition against Him was formal, with records (v. 2) and a plan (3:1-6).
- A slander campaign against Him began (3:22).
- The questioning and testing of Jesus began (8:11).
- The opposition drew His disciples into the conflict (9:14).
- The Pharisees came to test Him (10:2).
- Jesus cleansed the temple in anger (11:15-19).
- Jesus' authority was called into question (11:27-33).

After Jesus arrived in Jerusalem, the opposition accelerated. There were constant conflicts with every kind of religious official—Pharisees, Herodians, Sadducees, teachers of the law, chief priests and finally the Sanhedrin. They argued about every conceivable subject—taxes, marriage, washing hands, the resurrection, the nature of love, wealth and so on.

But behind all of the opposition, the motives were very clear:

- The chief priests and the teachers of the law heard this and began looking for a way to kill him, for they feared him (Mark 11:18).
- Then they looked for a way to arrest him because they knew he had spoken the parable against them (12:12).
- The chief priests and the teachers of the law were looking for some sly way to arrest Jesus and kill him (14:1).
- Then Judas Iscariot, one of the Twelve, went to the chief priests to betray Jesus to them. They were delighted to hear this and promised to give him money (14:10-11).
- The chief priests and the whole Sanhedrin were looking for evidence against Jesus so that they could put him to death (14:55).
- "Do you want me to release to you the king of the Jews?" asked Pilate, knowing it was out of envy that the chief priests had handed Jesus over to him (15:9-10).

The religious leadership rigidly reacted to Jesus and shaped its resposes into cold, hard, corrupt actions. And because it was so, Jesus had to confront it. As Stott has written:

> The popular image of Christ as "gentle Jesus, meek and mild" simply will not do. It is a false image. To be sure, he was full of love, compassion and tenderness. But he was also uninhibited in exposing error and denouncing sin, especially hypocrisy. Jesus was a controversialist.[2]

Beneath the many topics of controversy, one basic issue surfaced again and again—*authority*:

- The people were amazed at his teaching, because he taught them as one who had authority (Mark 1:22).
- The people were all so amazed that they asked each other, "What is this? A new teaching—and with authority!" (1:27).
- But that you may know that the Son of Man has authority (2:10).
- So the Son of Man is Lord even of the Sabbath (2:28).
- The teachers of the law and the elders came to him. "By what authority are you doing these things?" they asked. "And who gave you authority to do this?" (11:27-28).

The fact that Jesus turned the authority of religion back to God threatened the personal authority of the religious leaders. This is why they bombarded Him with questions, tried to undermine His character and eventually, planned His murder.

Mark recorded the clearest picture of this authority war. The story is one of hard categories and sharp conflict. The authority foundations for the two sides are easily identified.

Consider the chart on the next page.

But, how can tradition be elevated to rival the command of God? How can the wrong authority become lodged in someone's heart? It occurs through the *power of process*.

The steady growth of a tree can crack a sidewalk. A bad habit can enslave a life. In religion, the *power of process* flows through several stages:

It begins as a *personal opinion*.

But, through constant use, it becomes a *time-honored custom*.

And, as this custom is honored, it soon becomes a *sacred tradition*.

And, over the course of time, the tradition is fur
ther elevated to *infallible decree.*

The *power of process* is slow, but steady. The movement
from opinion to law is powerful and difficult to detect. It is a
hardening of the categories, and it causes many problems in
Christian life:

DEVOTION IS GIVEN TO TRADITION

Tradition can support the authority of God or oppose it. And
so, tradition must always be measured by the command of
God. If the tables are turned and tradition is elevated, then it
will slowly begin to set aside and nullify the will of God.
And the devotion that was once given to the commands of
God will begin to be given to the traditions of men.

WORSHIP BECOMES WORDS

Tradition can produce an elaborate lip service, but the only
thing that can reach the heart is the authority of God. Jesus
contrasted ceremony with reality, form with fact. He demonstrated that external religion is worse than useless if the

THE RELIGIOUS ESTABLISHMENT	JESUS
"The tradition of the elders" (7:3)	"The commands of God" (7:8)
"Many other traditions" (7:4)	"The commands of God" (7:9)
"The tradition of the elders" (7:5)	"The word of God" (7:13)
"Rules taught by men" (7:7)	
"Traditions of men" (7:8)	
"Your own traditions" (7:9)	
"Your tradition" (7:13)	

heart is not right. Only a religion of the heart is open to the will of God.

HEARTS BEGIN TO HARDEN

Rather than focus on the outside—clean hands, Jesus said to focus on the inside—clean heart. If deep convictions do not come from the authority of God, then the heart, detached from Him, will harden. And in that heart will grow, "evil thoughts, sexual immorality, theft, murder, adultery, greed, malice, deceit, lewdness, envy, slander, arrogance and folly" (Mark 7:21-22).

And human tradition has no real power against evil on the inside:

> Such regulations indeed have an appearance of wisdom...but they lack any value in restraining sensual indulgence (Col. 2:23).

FOR REFLECTION

1. Why did Jesus receive political, social and nationalistic opposition?

2. How and why did Jesus touch so many areas of life in His ministry?

3. In Mark 11, how did Jesus turn a political parade into a religious statement?

4. What is the significance of "Jerusalem" in Mark?

5. Why are hard hearts impenetrable by human tradition?

6. How does Mark show Jesus in conflict with custom and tradition?

7. With what customs and traditions in your religion might Jesus have conflict?

8. How can tradition be elevated to a point where it rivals the commands of God?

9. What causes a church to "harden its categories?"

10. How can a church turn its worship back from "lips" to "hearts?"

Notes
1. John R. W. Stott, *Christ the Controversialist* (Downers Grove, IL: InterVarsity Press, 1970), back cover.
2. Ibid., p. 49.

9

Believe Me

We have come to share in Christ if we hold firmly till
the end the confidence we had at first (Heb. 3:14).

Everyone is familiar with the story of the tortoise and the
hare. And everyone knows what made the tortoise a winner.
We know that it wasn't his good looks or his family heritage.
We know that it wasn't his political connections or his lucky
breaks. Persistence made him a winner.

But, at the same time, how many of us have looked at
someone we consider to be successful and said, "If I had her
clothes, or her figure, or her connections, I would be successful too." It is easy to recognize persistence in the animal story
and miss it in the human story.

Not to persevere, to quit, is becoming increasingly popular. If you start to sink, don't bail—jump. If things get out of
hand, don't resolve them—just throw in the towel.

A marriage hits a difficult time: "Let's just quit." A dream
is met with obstacles: "Let's just quit." Something you really
believe in becomes difficult: "Let's just quit." But, as Arthur

Clark once wrote, "A faith that cannot survive collision with the truth is not worth many regrets."[1]

When we come face-to-face with the truth, do we quit or do we persevere?

This question has been growing in the mind of Jesus. He doesn't question His own faith; He questions the faith of His followers. What will happen to the Twelve when the difficulties come? Will they endure or will they quit? These men who have followed so readily and believed so strongly—will their faith survive a collision with the truth?

Thus far in their relationship, Jesus has said, "Follow Me, observe Me, study Me and slowly begin to understand Me." He had given them the time and opportunity to understand. He had said, "Participate in My ministry in as much depth as you can."

They did. And to be with Him was exciting. To see the crowds excited them. Indirectly, the Twelve felt the praise showered on Jesus by all the people and often experienced the same astonishment expressed by the crowds.

The Twelve probably even took pleasure in those early conflicts with the religious officials. They enjoyed watching Jesus give answers and ask questions that would silence and astonish His critics. It was easy to be with Him then.

But, along the way, they began to brush against the real truth of His mission. They began to hear hints of the difficulties ahead.

- But the time will come when the bridegroom will be taken from them, and on that day they will fast (Mark 2:20).
- He who has ears to hear, let him hear (4:9).
- Consider carefully what you hear (4:24).
- They were terrified and asked each other, "Who is this?" (4:41).

- "Be careful," Jesus warned them. "Watch out for the yeast of the Pharisees and that of Herod" (8:15).

These were shades of what was ahead. Early hints of His death, His cross, His real mission. But now it is time for Jesus to speak directly and clearly. And, in three episodes, the faith of the Twelve collides with the truth, with reality.

EPISODE ONE—CAESAREA PHILIPPI

He then began to teach them that the Son of Man must suffer many things and be rejected by the elders, chief priests and teachers of the law, and that he must be killed and after three days rise again.

He spoke plainly about this, and Peter took him aside and began to rebuke him....

Then he called the crowd to him along with his disciples and said: "If anyone would come after me, he must deny himself and take up his cross and follow me" (Mark 8:31-32,34).

Jesus had been quiet about His identity for a long time. He knew that words and titles many times fail because they require that those listening have "ears to hear." And so, for months He had worked hard at *living His identity* for the Twelve to see.

Yet though His disciples *had seen* him continually give His time, His energy, His emotion and His very life for people, they did not see His ultimate goal. They did not see that His serving style led directly to the highest form of service—self-sacrifice.

Finally, Jesus spoke directly and clearly. In fact, He was so clear that He was difficult to hear. He said that the success of His mission required His death. This shattered the political and social aspirations of the Twelve.

At the very moment that Peter identified Jesus as the Christ, the Messiah (8:29), Jesus had said, in effect, "It's not what you think. Don't tell anyone. You don't understand" (8:30).

In part, Jesus was saying, "You believed in Me when it was easy, when it was popular, when it was exciting. But will you believe in Me now, knowing more of the story? Will you believe in Me when it's hard?"

And the Twelve were left with a decision: Would they continue to believe or not?

Jesus was speaking of something far deeper than giving things. To give things to God without really giving ourselves is only too easy.

Jesus wanted to be perfectly plain, so He didn't say, "You must deny yourself some *things*." The Twelve had already done that. Some of them had left their businesses. Some had left families. Some had left every kind of security to follow Jesus. In fact, Peter would later say, "We have left everything to follow you" (10:28).

But Jesus knew that the deepest faith went beyond denying yourself *things* to denying *yourself*. There is a kind of denial that can produce spiritual pride. Remember the Pharisee who boasted of his denials: "I tithe, I fast" (Luke 18:11-12). But notice what was still at the center: "*I*." Self had not been denied.

Jesus was speaking of something far deeper than giving things. To give *things* to God without really giving ourselves is only too easy. J. B. Phillips translates Mark 8:34, "He must give up all right to himself."

The word "deny" described Peter denying Jesus (14:68-72). The painful lesson is that, ultimately, we must choose one or the other. We must deny ourselves or deny Him.

EPISODE TWO—PASSING THROUGH GALILEE

They left that place and passed through Galilee. Jesus did not want anyone to know where they were, because he was teaching his disciples.

He said to them, "The Son of Man is going to be betrayed into the hands of men. They will kill him, and after three days he will rise."

But they did not understand what he meant and were afraid to ask him about it (Mark 9:30-32).

At this point, Jesus clearly was no longer the hero of Galilee. And equally clear was the fact that the Herodian government was out to kill Him (Luke 13:31). So after Jesus succeeded in avoiding the tremendous political pressure of the 5,000 patriots (Mark 6:30-44), widespread desertions began among His followers (John 6:66).

They were disappointed. Jesus would not be king. At least, not the kind of king they wanted.

Now, Jesus and the Twelve kept to the back roads. They crossed Galilee in secret spending more time alone. This particular meeting was deliberate and the isolation was planned.

You see, Jesus was preparing to leave. But He didn't concentrate on getting His own affairs in order. Instead, He focused on the Twelve. He prepared them. Would they continue to believe after He was gone?

Harry Emerson Fosdick wrote, "It is cynicism and fear

that freezes life; and it is faith that thaws it out, releases it, sets it free."[2]

Jesus had invested His time, His energy and His life in the Twelve. But to what end? Would their fear freeze the mission or would their faith carry it on?

EPISODE THREE—OUTSIDE JERUSALEM

They were on their way up to Jerusalem, with Jesus leading the way, and the disciples were astonished, while those who followed were afraid. Again he took the Twelve aside and told them what was going to happen to him.

"We are going up to Jerusalem," he said, "and the Son of Man will be betrayed to the chief priests and teachers of the law. They will condemn him to death and will hand him over to the Gentiles, who will mock him and spit on him, flog him and kill him. Three days later he will rise" (Mark 10:32-34).

There was tension in the air. The words "on their way up to Jerusalem" highlighted the goal of Jesus' determined journey. The description of Jesus "leading the way" pictured Him stepping out far ahead of the Twelve, completely immersed in His destiny. And the explanation of the disciples' attitude as "afraid" amplified the tension.

Picture the two groups: Jesus, a lonely figure walking out ahead, sure of His destiny, relentless in His mission. And the Twelve, astonished, afraid and lagging behind. The closer Jesus got to His cross, the more visible was the difference between His mission and theirs.

Three difficult episodes. Three predictions of death. And with each consecutive announcement, the picture grew grimmer:

- He makes the first shocking announcement that He is to be killed (Mark 8:31).
- He predicts the tragedy of betrayal (9:31).
- He details the torture and ridicule (10:34).

He was pacing the Twelve, giving them a little more each time. But even with the picture growing darker, and even when Jesus felt consumed with the task ahead (Luke 12:50), He remained true to His mission of training, educating and equipping the Twelve.

The Cross, His atoning death, was the center of His mission. But His mission must be reproduced in the Twelve or else it would all end at the Cross. His mission must be reproduced in Christians today. Our faith, which began with excitement, joy and confidence, must continue, especially as we get closer to the Cross.

There once lived a man in a great forest who spent his days cutting wood. He had stacked up huge walls of wood, enough to last him for years. And in his great library were many books on the purpose and use of fire. He had amassed all the tools and all the materials. Yet he was still cold, and he stayed in the cold because he had everything he needed except the spark.

Today we can amass tons of Christian tools and religious equipment. And yet we can lose "the confidence we had at first" (Heb. 3:14), that spark of faith which will ignite the Christian life. Will we continue to believe?

Ask yourself these questions:

- *Will I continue to believe when it's hard?* When the excitement has died down? When the difficulties are many?
- *Will I continue to believe when others do not?* When the crowds thin out? When others encourage me to quit? When I am tired?

- *Will I continue to believe when I don't completely under-stand?* When it goes against my own views?
- *Will I continue to believe when God doesn't seem to be there?* When I can't sense the presence of God? When I feel alone? When I don't understand how Jesus can be with me?

FOR REFLECTION

1. How has quitting become a life-style in today's culture?

2. How does Jesus express His concern for disciples who might quit?

3. What does Jesus require of me if I am to be successful in my mission?

4. In what ways do you identify with Peter and his total willingness to follow Jesus, plus his lack of belief?

5. How is self-denial related to deep faith?

6. Can Jesus be absolutely certain that after He has invested His time and energy in the Twelve, that they will continue His mission?

7. What kinds of things cause you to have the greatest doubts?

8. When is it really hard for you to continue to follow Jesus?

9. What are three practical things you can do to keep from quitting Jesus?

10. Why is it tempting to leave Jesus when life goes against us?

Notes
1. Tony Castle, ed., *The New Book of Christian Quotations* (New York: The Crossroad Publishing Co., 1988), p. 82.
2. Ibid.

10
Pray with Me

Distance is a subject of science, transportation and communication. We use it to measure how far people, continents and
planets are from each other. Most of the time distance is a
physical measurement.

But physical measurement is not the only way to consider
distance. There are also social and economic distances, moral
and political distances, racial and religious distances, emotional and psychological distances. In fact, one small area of a
city may contain both wealth and poverty, education and
ignorance, security and fear. And though the physical distance separating people is small, the social, emotional and
spiritual distance can be overwhelming.

It has often been said that our world is shrinking. The
speed of transportation and communication is making the
physical distance between cities and continents insignificant.
Yet our world must not be measured only by the size of its
technological advances, but also by the size of its problems.

As the world shrinks, the distance between people grows
larger. Individuals can live in the same house, and yet never

speak. They can live in the same neighborhood and be afraid of each other.

And so, on one level, we measure distance in units of miles and hours. In deeper dimensions we measure it with poverty levels, stress factors and personality profiles.

Yet there is an even deeper dimension in human life, an even more profound distance to measure. It is the distance between right and wrong, loyalty and betrayal, integrity and hypocrisy. Physical measurements will pass away, but the distance between light and darkness is timeless. This eternal dimension is not measured in hours or miles. Jesus showed us that it is measured in units of prayer.

A Praying Man

Jesus prayed often. The Gospels record many occasions of prayer:

- At His baptism (Luke 3:21).
- Before choosing His Apostles (6:12-16).
- Before breaking the news of His death (9:18-22).
- On the Mount of Transfiguration (9:28).
- Before teaching His disciples to pray (11:1-4).
- After the seventy-two returned with a report of their mission (10:21-22).
- Before walking on the sea (Matt. 14:23-25).
- Before raising Lazarus (John 11:41-42).
- At the Passover feast (17:1-26).
- In the Garden of Gethsemane (Matt. 26:36-42; Luke 22:39-46).
- On the Cross (Matt. 27:46; Luke 23:46).

No doubt we could add to this list other prayers that were never recorded (John 21:25). Clearly prayer was an important part of His daily life. Leaving heaven was like leaving home.

The distance was enormous. And when life became demanding and difficult, prayer was His link back to His Father:

> During the days of Jesus' life on earth, he offered up prayers and petitions with loud cries and tears (Heb. 5:7).

However, the Gospel of Mark doesn't mention all of the prayers of Jesus. In fact, it alludes to very few and, among them, chooses to focus on only three. Among the many times Jesus prayed, why did Mark highlight these three? Because each is a turning point, a crisis and a progressively more difficult decision.

Mark focused on them to show the struggles in Jesus' life. He wanted to demonstrate that Jesus too had the choice of right or wrong. He too stood in the gap between loyalty and betrayal, integrity and hypocrisy. And for Him, the distance between a good decision and a bad one was measured in units of prayer.

LOCAL CRISIS

> Very early in the morning, while it was still dark, Jesus got up, left the house and went off to a solitary place, where he prayed. Simon and his companions went to look for him, and when they found him, they exclaimed: "Everyone is looking for you!"
>
> Jesus replied, "Let us go somewhere else—to the nearby villages—so I can preach there also. That is why I have come."
>
> So he traveled throughout Galilee, preaching in their synagogues and driving out demons (Mark 1:35-39).

Beyond any doubt, Galileans considered Jesus to be a local hero. The word about Him was spreading quickly. Everyone was talking about this Jesus. He was a popular, sought-after celebrity:

• The people were amazed (Mark 1:22).
• The people were all so amazed (1:27).
• Evil spirits...obey him (1:27).
• Jesus healed many (1:34).

The pace of Jesus' ministry was long and exhausting. It began early and lasted all day. So Jesus had to get up "very early" in order to have some time a lone with His Father.

When Simon Peter went to search for Jesus, he and his companions represented the search of "everyone." The needs were so many and so great, Jesus could easily have stayed in Galilee for the rest of His life. And that concern was the essence of this local crisis. Would Jesus remain in Galilee—or would He continue His mission?

The Greek word *katadioko* (Mark 1:36) used to describe the search for Jesus is a strong one. It means "hunted down" or "tracked down." All occurrences in Mark echo Satan's attempt to distract, deter or destroy Jesus or to change Jesus' picture of what His mission should be (3:32; 8:11; 11:18; 12:12; 14:1,11,55).

And so, in a time of crisis, the distance between Jesus and the Twelve is measured in getting up early and finding time alone with God. For Jesus, prayer was not simply a place to make requests, but also a place to make decisions. He prayed, then made His decision—and immediately the pace resumed.

Popularity lost to obedience.

NATIONAL CRISIS

The number of the men who had eaten was five thousand.
Immediately Jesus made his disciples get into the boat and go on ahead of him to Bethsaida, while he dismissed the crowd. After leaving them, he went up on a mountainside to pray (Mark 6:44-46).

Jesus had earlier sent the Twelve out on a mission of healing and teaching (Mark 6:7-13). But when they returned, with them was a large crowd eventually numbering 5,000 men.

In a national crisis, the distance between Jesus and the army of patriots is seen in the fact that they wanted to eat and fight, while He wanted to pray.

Jesus had instructed the Twelve to spend their mission preaching repentance and healing, but is that *all* they had done?

What about the 5,000? John reports that the crowd had come to make Jesus king *"by force"* (John 6:15). This was not a chance crowd, but the beginnings of a nationalistic rebellion.

Seeing the crowd and perceiving their purpose, Jesus immediately thought of the Old Testament phrase, *"sheep without a shepherd."* This pastoral expression was among many consistently used to picture the nation of Israel as being without a political leader (Num. 27:17; 1 Kings 22:17; 2 Chron. 18:16; Ps. 78:70-72; Isa. 44:28; 63:11; Ezek. 34:1-5; Zech. 10:2; 11:4-17).

According to Numbers 27, Moses prayed that God would raise up a man to lead the nation of Israel *"so the Lord's people will not be like sheep without a shepherd"* (v. 17). This incident also took place in a solitary place and the man chosen was *"Joshua,"* the Hebrew equivalent of *"Jesus."* Jesus did see Himself as a shepherd (John 10:11), but His style of leadership was clashing with the political expectations of both the Twelve and the 5,000 men they had gathered.

Once again a major decision faced Jesus. Would He give in to the pressure to bring power back to Israel? Or would He remain true to His Father's mission?

Jesus knew that He would not be the kind of military leader that Joshua had been in times past. So He began to disarm the army. He dismissed the crowd and *"forced"* (Mark 6:45) the Twelve to leave. And there, in a national crisis, the distance between Jesus and the army of patriots is seen in the fact that they wanted to eat and fight, while He wanted to pray.

Universal Crisis

They went to a place called Gethsemane, and Jesus said to his disciples, "Sit here while I pray."

He took Peter, James and John along with him, and he began to be deeply distressed and troubled. "My soul is overwhelmed with sorrow to the point of death," he said to them. "Stay here and keep watch."

Going a little farther, he fell to the ground and prayed that if possible the hour might pass from him. "Abba, Father," he said, "everything is possible for you. Take this cup from me. Yet not what I will, but what you will" (Mark 14:32-36).

In the local crisis, Jesus had to decide between two good options: Would He confine His teaching and healing ministry to Galilee or would He follow a wider mission? He made His decision in prayer.

In the national crisis, the choices were clearer but more difficult. The 5,000 patriots thought that it would be very good for Jesus to become king. The pressure to satisfy so many must have been great. Again, Jesus made His decision in prayer.

Jesus found each successive decision more difficult than the previous one. And the agony of His prayers reflected this increasing tension. These crises, with their progressively difficult choices and decisions, had the effect of preparing Jesus for the most difficult decision of all—in a universal crisis.

Jesus knew that the agents of evil were gathering. Judas had betrayed Him. His theological enemies had begun making plans to capture Him. A murderous mob had started forming against Him. What distance lay between Jesus and these instruments of evil?

A stone's throw away the Twelve slept. Depression and confusion had drained them. They didn't understand why Jesus had consistently resisted any part in their political plans. Their efforts to convince Him had only left them frustrated and *"exhausted from sorrow"* (Luke 22:45). What distance lay between Jesus and His sleeping team?

Not far away awaited two trials. Jesus would be taken before the Sanhedrin—and later before Pilate. Lies would be told. Fear and panic would overrule truth. What was the distance between this legal sham, where justice was forgotten and Jesus, whose death would satisfy the justice of the eternal God?

The distance was measured in units of prayer. Jesus did what He had always done: He made His decision in prayer. Then He arose, woke His disciples, met His enemies and completed His mission.

"Enough! The hour has come. Look, the Son of Man is

betrayed into the hands of sinners. Rise! Let us go! Here comes my betrayer!" (Mark 14:41-42).

> Prayer is a shield to the soul,
> a sacrifice to God,
> and a scourge to Satan.[1]

For Jesus, prayer was a place to make decisions. It was a time to offer Himself as the answer to His own prayers. Prayer is the distance between those who consistently do the will of God and those who don't.

FOR REFLECTION

1. Why was Jesus a "praying man"?

2. How was Jesus' view of prayer different from the view held by the religious leaders of His day?

3. When you were growing up, what did you think about the Lord's Prayer?

4. When is it easy for you to pray? When is it difficult and what is the difference?

5. Why do people stop praying?

6. What qualities are required for an effective prayer life?

7. Is it easy or difficult for you to pray in a time of crisis? Why or why not?

8. What are some practical steps you can take to close the distance between you and Jesus?

9. How did Jesus use prayer as a place to make decisions?

10. Can you picture Jesus praying for you? How does it make you feel?

Note
1. John Bunyan, *The New Book of Christian Quotations* (New York: The Crossroad Publishing Company, 1988), p. 190.

11
Suffer with Me

- The elderly couple, well into their 80s, were so frail, they could hardly walk unaided into the church building. Still every time they taught, their classes were overflowing with those waiting to hear them. The old brother could barely speak above a whisper, yet men would strain to hear him. And his wife always filled her ladies' class with women eager to learn.

  What was the old couple's special quality? It was partly their longevity, but more particularly their suffering. These credentials gave their witness an authority that influenced and inspired the hearts of other people.
- Though a relatively young man, Bill's cancer usually confined him to bed. Still, Christians would go to his house to seek his advice. They admired the way that—despite his debilitating illness—he had used his financial success to turn his home into a place of Christian service to others. Homeless people, recover-

ing drug addicts and former prostitutes all were welcome there.

Bill taught them and brought them to Jesus. In the year before he died, Bill was constantly invited to address groups in the medical community on death and dying. His suffering had given him special authority in his community.

Suffering bestows an undefinable, yet tangible authority upon those who have experienced it. That stamp of authority

---

It was Jesus' involvement in human suffering that led those observing Him to conclude that He spoke and acted with authority.

---

demonstrates what such persons have been through. It reveals what they have endured.

Such authority sometimes commands the kind of respect accorded an athlete because of his lengthy and painful training. At other times it brings the honor granted to a scholar because of her diligent study. It also wins accolades from a grateful nation for the serviceman or woman who at, great personal cost, turns certain defeat into victory.

But more often, though unheralded, authority cloaks the widow speaking to another woman who has just lost her husband. That same authority resides in the man confined to a wheelchair who gives courage to a young boy newly paralyzed in an automobile accident. It fills a hospital corridor where a man who has buried his son holds a weeping father whose daughter has just died.

We say of these people, "They know what they are talking about." Because they have known suffering and are not merely detached observers, they have a special right to be heard. And because they are themselves wounded healers, they have the authority to help others who are wounded in body and in spirit.

People sensed authority in Jesus. It set Him apart from other teachers and religious leaders. Mark highlights His authority early in his Gospel story (emphasis added):

- The people were amazed at his teaching, because he taught them as one who had *authority* (1:22).
- The people were all so amazed that they asked each other, "What is this? A new teaching—and with *authority!*" (1:27).
- "But that you may know that the Son of Man has *authority* on earth to forgive sins...." He said to the paralytic, "I tell you, get up, take your mat and go home" (2:10-11).

But as the story unfolds, paralleling Jesus' authority was His ever-deepening involvement in human suffering. Whether it was His delivering the demon-possessed (1:32-34), cleansing the leper (1:40), healing the paralytic (2:1-12) or fellowshiping with the social outcast (2:15-17), Jesus opened himself up to their sufferings. In fact, it was Jesus' involvement in human suffering that led those observing Him to conclude that He spoke and acted with authority.

That the proof of Jesus' authority was His involvement in suffering is what the Hebrew letter refers to when it states (emphasis added):

- Although he was a son, he learned obedience from what he *suffered* and, once made perfect, he became

the source of eternal salvation for all who obey him
(5:8-9).

• In bringing many sons to glory, it was fitting that God,
for whom and through whom everything exists,
should make the author of their salvation perfect
through *suffering* (2:10).

• Because he himself *suffered* when he was tempted, he is
able to help those who are being tempted (2:18).

In Paul's letter to the Philippian church, it is no coinci-
dence that, following that ancient hymn describing Jesus'
descent into human suffering, comes a tremendous description of His authority:

> Therefore God exalted him to the highest place
> and gave him the name that is above every name,
> that at the name of Jesus every knee should bow, in
> heaven and on earth and under the earth, and every
> tongue confess that Jesus Christ is Lord, to the glory
> of God the Father (Phil. 2:9-11).

Lordship followed crucifixion. Authority followed suffering. The One who "emptied himself" (Phil. 2:7, *RSV*) is the
One whose authority will be recognized by "every knee" and
"every tongue."

Because He was painfully aware of His own suffering,
Jesus had a special right to speak. Especially did He have this
right when He explained to His disciples that they will suffer:

> You must be on your guard. You will be handed over
> to the local councils and flogged in the synagogues.
> On account of me you will stand before governors
> and kings as witnesses to them.

And the gospel must first be preached to all nations.

Whenever you are arrested and brought to trial, do not worry beforehand about what to say. Just say whatever is given you at the time, for it is not you speaking, but the Holy Spirit.

Brother will betray brother to death, and a father his child. Children will rebel against their parents and have them put to death. All men will hate you because of me, but he who stands firm to the end will be saved (Mark 13:9-13).

Four times in Mark 13, Jesus warns His disciples to be watchful and to stay on their guard. After being very clear about His own suffering, He was leaving no doubt that to choose Him is to choose a hard way.

In fact, He predicted three occasions of suffering (v. 9): "You will be handed over to the *local councils*....you will stand before *governors* and *kings* as witnesses to them." And all three of them came to pass:

- **Local Councils.** Having brought the apostles, they made them appear before *the Sanhedrin*....

  They called the apostles in and had them flogged. Then they ordered them not to speak in the name of Jesus, and let them go.

  The apostles left *the Sanhedrin*, rejoicing because they had been counted worthy of suffering disgrace for the Name (Acts 5:27,40-41).
- **Governors.** They brought their charges against Paul before *the governor*. When Paul was called in, Tertullus presented his case before Felix....When two years had passed, Felix was succeeded by Porcius Festus,

but because Felix wanted to grant a favor to the Jews, he left Paul in prison (Acts 24:1-2,27).

- **Kings.** The next day Agrippa and Bernice came with great pomp and entered the audience room with the high ranking officers and the leading men of the city. At the command of Festus, Paul was brought in. Festus said: *"King Agrippa,* and all who are present with us, you see this man! The whole Jewish community has petitioned me about him in Jerusalem and here in Caesarea, shouting that he ought not to live any longer" (Acts 25:23-24).

It all came to pass. But why were these early Christians attracting this kind of suffering? One sentence makes it all perfectly clear:

> When they saw the courage of Peter and John and realized that they were unschooled, ordinary men, they were astonished and they took note that these men had been *with Jesus* (Acts 4:13, emphasis added).

These early Christians had learned about the authority of suffering from Jesus. Tradition tells us that only one of the Twelve apostles died of old age. The others met with violent deaths: Among them, Stephen, a deacon from the Jerusalem church, was stoned. Matthew died a martyr's death in Ethiopia. Andrew and Peter were crucified. Paul was beaten eight times and shipwrecked three times before being decapitated outside of Rome.

It was illegal to be a Christian during the first three centuries of Church history. The early Church was slandered during that time. Christians were called atheists because they didn't believe in the Roman gods. They were said to be cannibals because of a twisted understanding of the Lord's Supper. All in all, they were handy scapegoats. Now, we can look back to the eighth beatitude with deeper understanding: "Blessed are those who are persecuted because of righteousness" (Matt. 5:10).

In a time of heated baptistries, air-conditioned auditoriums and padded pews, can we understand the authority of suffering? What does it mean to be a wounded healer today? Consider these lessons:

The real issue is not, Will I suffer?
Jesus was definite and certain: Suffering
is inevitable.

SUFFERING REQUIRES AN ETERNAL VIEWPOINT

The perspective of the Twelve was limited and immediate: "What massive stones! What magnificent buildings!" (Mark 13:1). They were impressed with the here and now, so Jesus immediately broadened their narrow viewpoint to include what would happen in the future: "Not one stone here will be left on another; every one will be thrown down" (13:2).

In fact, this entire chapter is future-oriented. The discussion moved from persecution to the destruction of Jerusalem to the end of the world. And Jesus called all of this turmoil, "the beginning of birth pains" (13:8).

They would be a part of something much bigger. Jesus pushed the discussion to the end of time and, by the end of this chapter, said, in effect, that ministry is much bigger than the trouble it brings. So "keep watch, be alert, be on guard" (see v. 37).

SUFFERING GIVES AUTHORITY TO MINISTRY

In the middle of His discussion about suffering, Jesus said, "The gospel must first be preached to all nations" (13:10). Ministry will take place in the midst of suffering. And the suffering gives credibility to that ministry. Reflecting on how Jesus demonstrated this truth on the Cross, Peter wrote:

> When they hurled their insults at him, he did not retaliate; when he suffered, he made no threats. Instead, he entrusted himself to him who judges justly. He himself bore our sins in his body on the tree, so that we might die to sins and live for righteousness; by his wounds you have been healed (1 Pet. 2:23-24).

This wounded healer had great credibility and, therefore, great authority. Paul put it this way:

> If we are distressed, it is for your comfort and salvation; if we are comforted, it is for your comfort, which produces in you patient endurance of the same sufferings we suffer.
>
> And our hope for you is firm, because we know that just as you share in our sufferings, so also you share in our comfort (2 Cor. 1:6-7).

Suffering can drive a person to discouragement or it can give him the authority to serve.

SUFFERING IS UNAVOIDABLE

The real issue is not, Will I suffer? Jesus was definite and certain on this point: Suffering is inevitable.

The real issue is: What will suffering contribute to my life? Will it destroy me? Will it discourage me? Or will it give my life authority to help, to serve and to heal?

Jesus didn't want the Twelve to prepare speeches. He wanted them to prepare themselves. So He instructed them, "Whenever you are arrested...do not worry beforehand about what to say" (Mark 13:11).

The best preparation is not detailed arrangements, specific plans or a finished speech. Our best preparation is much deeper. It is the provision we have made inside. Only this will enable us to stand "firm to the end" (13:13).

FOR REFLECTION

1. Name someone you have known who has suffered for Jesus.

2. How does the suffering of Jesus give Him authority?

3. List at least three examples in which Jesus involved Himself in human suffering?

4. How does the suffering of Jesus give Him a special right to speak and be heard?

5. How did Jesus prepare Himself and the Twelve for suffering?

6. How do you understand the words of Jesus, "Blessed are those who are persecuted for righteousness' sake" (Matt. 5:10, RSV)?

7. What kind of perspective does suffering require? Why?

8. What is the best preparation for suffering?

9. How does suffering relate to ministering to people?

10. How and to what degree have you "felt the heat" because of your faith in Jesus?

12

Remember Me

Our culture has many ways to commemorate the life of someone who has passed on. For the private person, a simple tombstone with a name, a date and perhaps an inscription is a typical commemoration. For the public person, a monument or a statue may be raised to honor the deceased. For the wealthy person, sometimes a lectureship or a scholarship is established or even a building erected bearing his or her name.

Those left behind are normally the ones who choose the form of the memorial. This is the usual way the dead are memorialized. What is unusual is for a person to anticipate his own death with enough time to plan his own memorial.

Jesus was such a person. Yet no monuments or statues were in His memorial plans. He hasn't even a marked grave of any certainty. And though the Church bears His name, it is unlike other institutions in the way it remembers its founder. For the memorial that Jesus took great care to plan was just a simple, thoughtful, frequent meal.

While they were eating, Jesus took bread, gave thanks and broke it, and gave it to his disciples, saying, "Take it; this is my body."

Then he took the cup, gave thanks and offered it to them, and they all drank from it. "This is my blood of the covenant, which is poured out for many," he said to them. "I tell you the truth, I will not drink again of the fruit of the vine until that day when I drink it anew in the kingdom of God."

When they had sung a hymn, they went out to the Mount of Olives (Mark 14:22-26).

We keep the memory alive because He is alive. And so, we encounter Jesus, not because He is more present in the Supper than at any other time, but because, in the Supper, we are more aware.

We are all familiar with this simple Supper which Christians continue to share today. But the story that we rehearse each week is so familiar to us that sometimes it brings no emotion or thoughtful introspection. For some it doesn't even require thought. Like typing or walking, the habit has become routine and the routine has become reflex.

But the Lord's Supper is not a routine task. In fact, the reason for the habit is to keep the memory fresh and the reflections growing. The memorial is repeated so that our understanding can be deepened each time we observe it.

We keep the memory alive because He is alive. And so,

we encounter Jesus, not because He is more present in the Supper than at any other time, but because, in the Supper, we are more aware. This frequent Supper becomes meaningful when we decide to rescue the memory from routine.

Today, we live in a time of comfort and peace as we try to remember back to a time of violence and death. And it is tempting to see Jesus' Last Supper as the calm before the storm. But the real story is different.

The storm had begun much earlier. Notice the painful context within which the Supper is set (emphasis added):

- The chief priests and the teachers of the law were looking for some sly way to *arrest* Jesus and *kill* him (Mark 14:1).
- She poured perfume on my body beforehand to prepare for my *burial* (14:8).
- Judas Iscariot...went to the chief priests to *betray* Jesus to them. They were delighted to hear this and promised to give him money. So he watched for an opportunity to hand him over (14:10-11).
- I tell you the truth, one of you will *betray* me (14:18).
- You will all *fall away* (14:27).
- Before the rooster crows twice you yourself will *disown* me three times (14:30).
- When he came back, he again found them *sleeping* (14:40).
- Now the *betrayer* had arranged a signal with them: "The one I kiss is the man; *arrest* him and lead him away under guard" (14:44).
- Then everyone *deserted* him and fled (14:50).
- Many *testified falsely* against him (14:56).
- But he *denied* it. "I don't know or understand what you're talking about" (14:68).

- Again he *denied* it (14:70).
- He began to call down curses on himself, and he *swore* to them, "I don't know this man you're talking about" (14:71).

Amazingly, it was in a context of desertion, denial and betrayal that Jesus instituted His own memorial. Planning for memory was just too important to be put off by the failure of others. But what kind of memorial is it?

The death of a man usually puts him in the past. But the Resurrection has brought Jesus dramatically into the future....At the Supper we eat, drink and remember, for tomorrow we live.

INTROSPECTIVE—REMEMBERING NOW

The story of the Last Supper is sandwiched in between *predictions* of desertion, denial and betrayal and *actual* desertion, denial and betrayal. Jesus amazes us by His sharing an intimate meal, usually reserved for special family and friends, with the Twelve. He knew what was ahead for them—and for Himself. And still He shared the Supper.

The same is true even now. Tarnished with today's betrayal, we bring our true selves to the Supper. We can't pretend to leave our failure outside. We bring it to the only One who has an answer.

Actually, sin was not just Judas' problem. "You will all fall away," Jesus said to the Twelve (Mark 14:27), not just to

Judas. Still, Judas symbolizes the sin that's in every heart—
my heart, your heart. And at the Supper, we are called to a
heart-searching introspection.

RETROSPECTIVE—REMEMBERING THE PAST

Human beings forget. We forget names, events and promises.
And so Jesus said, "Do this in remembrance of me" (Luke
22:19). Do what? Remember what?

The Bread

Jesus first took bread and made it a symbol of His body. A
body that would be scourged, beaten and abused. A body
that would be nailed, bloodied and killed. A body that
would be buried and then given life and resurrection.

So when He said, "This is my body" (Mark 14:22), He
meant, "This is My person." And today, when we share the
bread, we join ourselves to His person, His cause and His
values.

The Wine

Next, Jesus took wine and made it a symbol of His blood: the
blood that would cover His head, His hands, His feet, His
side and His back. He said, "This is my blood of the
covenant, which is poured out for many" (Mark 14:24).

Today, when we share the cup, we include ourselves in
the "many." We look back and thank God for the blood
which daily purifies us of our guilt.

The Towel and Basin

Finally, Jesus took a towel and basin. And at this point we see
His priorities. He must have given deep thought to what His
final message to the Twelve would be. Therefore, when the

disciples last saw Jesus at work, they saw Him in the role of a servant.

And so, retrospection is a time to thank God for the broken body, the shed blood and the forgiven life. But retrospection is also a time to decide again to follow Jesus in service. "I have set you an example that you should do as I have done for you" (John 13:15).

PROSPECTIVE—REMEMBER THE FUTURE

"For whenever you eat this bread and drink this cup, you proclaim the Lord's death until he comes" (1 Cor. 11:26). This is sometimes called "the already but not yet." The Lord is coming again. And when we observe the Supper, we remember the future.

But how can we remember forward? We have difficulty because we think chronologically about a God who is beyond chronology. He created time. He is above time. He is beyond time.

The death of a man usually puts him in the past. But the Resurrection has brought Jesus dramatically into the future. The world says, "Eat, drink and be merry, for tomorrow we die." But at the Supper we *eat, drink* and *remember*, for tomorrow we *live*.

And so, we look inward, backward and forward.

But still, why a meal? Why didn't Jesus build a monument of stone? Why is a meal an appropriate memorial to Jesus?

There are good reasons:

IN THE SUPPER WE ENCOUNTER A RISEN LORD

Monuments are usually built by people who are left behind at the time of someone's death. The Jefferson Memorial. The

Washington Monument. The Lincoln Memorial. Who built these monuments? They were built by those who were left behind after these great men died.

We cannot go to a marked grave today and worship Jesus, because He is not in a grave. He has risen!

IN THE SUPPER WE ENCOUNTER ONE ANOTHER

In the Supper, Christians share an experience. When we eat the Supper, we are not only in a vertical relationship with Jesus, but we are also in a horizontal relationship with each other. We don't eat alone. This is why Paul rebuked the Corinthian Christians for their observance of the Supper:

> I have no praise for you, for your meetings do more harm than good. In the first place, I hear that when you come together as a church, there are divisions among you....
>
> As you eat, each of you goes ahead without waiting for anybody else....
>
> Anyone who eats and drinks *without recognizing the body of the Lord* eats and drinks judgment on himself (1 Cor. 11:17-18,21,29, emphasis added).

The term "body" is used 23 times in 1 Corinthians 10-12. The vast majority of these occurrences refer to the Church. In fact, in his warning against idolatry, Paul used "body" in a double sense, referring to both the physical body of Jesus and the spiritual Body—the Church:

> And is not the bread that we break a participation in the body of Christ? Because there is one loaf, we, who are many, are one body, for we all partake of the one loaf (1 Cor. 10:16-17).

In the Supper, we should *recognize* , *discern* and *comprehend* that we are in relationship with all other members of the Body.

The memory of that Last Supper brings to mind the balance in the life of Jesus: the balance of bread and wine, towel and basin, worship and service. When He died He was given no marble statue, no special sculpture, not even an epitaph—only a mocking inscription placed above His head on the Cross that bore the "charge" against Him (see Mark 15:26).

At the time it seemed that few would care or remember. But for 2,000 years, literally millions have gathered regularly to obey the command, "Remember Me."

FOR REFLECTION

1. What is unique about the "monuments" Jesus leaves behind?

2. Why do we need monuments to remember Jesus?

3. Explain how the Lord's Supper looks backward, forward and inward?

4. Why is the Lord's Supper—as opposed to a building or statue—an appropriate monument to Jesus?

5. What are we to think about while partaking of the Lord's Supper?

6. Explain the vertical and horizontal relationships of the Lord's Supper?

7. What does the "body" refer to in 1 Corinthians 11:29?

8. What does it mean to "discern the body"?

9. How do Christians perpetuate the Spirit and life of Jesus?

10. What are some practical steps that Christians can take to improve the *way* we participate in the Lord's Supper?

13

Preach Me

When the Sabbath was over, Mary Magdalene, Mary
the mother of James, and Salome bought spices so
that they might go to anoint Jesus' body....

As they entered the tomb, they saw a young man
dressed in a white robe sitting on the right side, and
they were alarmed.

"Don't be alarmed," he said. "You are looking for
Jesus the Nazarene, who was crucified. He has risen!
He is not here. See the place where they laid him. But
go, tell his disciples and Peter, 'He is going ahead of
you into Galilee'" (Mark 16:1, 5-7).

The time that Jesus spent in Galilee was a period of great
popularity, the honeymoon of His ministry. He encountered
crowds of amazed followers and performed spectacular mir-
acles there. He was a local hero. Shunned by the religious
establishment, Galilee was thought to be too unorthodox and
too Gentile to produce anything good. Nevertheless, it was
where Jesus' ministry began:

- After John was put in prison, Jesus went *into Galilee,* proclaiming the good news of God (Mark 1:14).
- News about him spread quickly over the whole region *of Galilee* (1:28).

It was in the hills of Galilee that Jesus chose the Twelve and began their training. Since that time, His ministry had taken them out of Galilee, all over Palestine and eventually to Jerusalem where Jesus was killed. It was in Jerusalem that Jesus spoke of a final Galilee experience:

> "You will all fall away," Jesus told them, "for it is written: 'I will strike the shepherd, and the sheep will be scattered.' But after I have risen, I will go ahead of you *into Galilee*" (Mark 14:27-28).

The Shepherd who was struck down did return to Galilee to reassemble His scattered flock. After the trauma and tragedy of Jerusalem, Jesus wanted to go back to the place where His ministry began. He wanted to return to the honeymoon site, where the memories were good. He wanted the apostles to connect the excitement of their first Galilee encounter with the power of their last—Resurrection.

At their first encounter, their zealous following was misguided. They followed their own political agenda and preached their own message. Jesus had told them many times about His resurrection (Mark 8:31; 9:9,31; 10:34), but their own view overruled and prevented them from understanding:

- Peter took him aside and began to rebuke him (Mark 8:32).
- They kept the matter to themselves, discussing what "rising from the dead" meant (Mark 9:10).
- But they did not understand what he meant and were afraid to ask him about it (9:32).

And so Jesus took them through a period of training that broke their hearts and dashed their political dreams. He took them through the fires of reality to emerge on the other side of death. They had never seen the other side of death until they witnessed the resurrected Jesus.

Earlier He had told them:

> Unless a kernel of wheat *falls* to the ground and *dies*, it remains only a single seed. But if it *dies*, it produces many seeds (John 12:24).

So, on the other side of His death, Jesus prepared the Twelve to sow the "many seeds" of His resurrection. He prepared them to preach:

> Later Jesus appeared to the Eleven as they were eating; he rebuked them for their lack of faith and their stubborn refusal to believe those who had seen him after he had risen.
>
> He said to them, "Go into all the world and preach the good news to all creation. Whoever believes and is baptized will be saved, but whoever does not believe will be condemned" (Mark 16:14-16).

In the beginning, Galilee had been a place of preparation. At the end, it became the springboard of mission.

Notice Jesus' final instructions:

THE MESSENGERS

After appearing to hundreds of His followers individually and in groups, "Jesus appeared to the Eleven" (Mark 16:14). In fact, the Great Commission is directed "to them" (Mark 16:15). Because of this fact, some have concluded that this mission was given strictly to the apostles alone.

After all, they were the eye-witnesses. They were the specially trained disciples. And so, quite naturally, they were the ones equipped to be the messengers.

Today this mentality shows itself in a clergy/laity separation, where the "hired gun" carries the message, while the rest watch. Some even say, "I'm not a trained minister. Leave ministry to the professionals." The unstated assumption behind this view is that the Eleven were highly trained professionals, ready to pick up where Jesus left off.

But is this assumption accurate? Look back through the story again:

- Do you have eyes but fail to see, and ears but fail to hear? (Mark 8:18).
- You do not have in mind the things of God, but the things of men (8:33).
- You will all fall away (14:27).
- Then everyone deserted him and fled (14:50).
- They did not believe (16:11).
- He rebuked them for their lack of faith (16:14).

Highly trained professionals? Specially equipped disciples? Would you leave your mission in the hands of these men? Jesus did!

Jesus confidently made the apostles His messengers. But His confidence did not rest in their superhuman abilities or spotless track record. No—His confidence was in the work His Father had done in the Resurrection.

And since the answer to death was resurrection, Jesus knew that the answer to hard-hearted, short-sighted disciples would be the same. He was confident that through the power of the Resurrection the apostles could carry His mission. They did!

A few days later the Eleven returned to Jerusalem—that

city of tragedy and trauma. They stood up in the courts and confidently preached the death, burial and resurrection of Jesus:

> Men of Israel, listen to this:
> Jesus of Nazareth was a man accredited by God to you by miracles, wonders and signs, which God did among you through him....This man was handed over to you by God's set purpose and foreknowledge; and you, with the help of wicked men, put him to death by nailing him to the cross.
> But God raised him from the dead, freeing him from the agony of death, because it was impossible for death to keep its hold on him (Acts 2:22-24).

There was no special skill or training that made the Eleven uniquely responsible to carry out the Great Commission. They had experienced discouragement and failure like the rest of us. But they came through their failure trusting in the power of the Resurrection (cf. Eph. 1:18-23).

They eventually learned that it is not the absence of failure that qualifies a person to be God's messenger. God has always entrusted great tasks to those who have handled great failure. God's messengers are those who have opened their eyes to the power of the Resurrection.

They see that resurrection power is not only the answer to their last enemy—death (1 Cor. 15:26), but also to their daily enemy—failure (Eph. 2:1,4-6). They qualify for ministry when they stop trusting in their own power and begin to trust in God's power.

THE MISSION

Sending the Eleven into the world with the most important mission ever given might seem to be a curious cure for a "lack of faith" and a "stubborn refusal to believe" (Mark 16:14). But they were not only learning to trust in God's power rather than their own, they were also learning to relinquish their own mission and take up His.

From the very beginning the apostles had seen Jesus as an opportunity to fulfill their own dreams and ambitions. He was their ticket to greatness. Through Him, they could get in on the ground-floor of a new Jewish kingdom (Mark 10:35-45). But instead of achieving their mission, they saw it destroyed. Rather than obtain cabinet member status in a new kingdom, they became outcasts in a crushed rebellion. Afraid and disillusioned they could only conclude that their mission had failed.

It was at this point that Jesus began to do for them what He does for us all. Once the failure of their own mission had opened their eyes and softened their hearts, they began to see the mission that Jesus had been teaching and modeling for them all along. He dealt with them individually (John 20:24-29; 21:15-19) and as a group (Matt. 28:16).

At least three times He appeared to the disciples (John 21:14). Each meeting was a time of confrontation, forgiveness and reinstatement. And each time He gave them His mission—preach the good news (Mark 16:15), make disciples (Matt. 28:19), feed my sheep (John 21:17), baptize and teach (Matt. 28:19-20).

"As you are going" more correctly interprets the meaning of the participle "go" (Mark 16:15; Matt. 28:19) and it describes Jesus' own style of ministry. He carried out His mission as He was going—as He walked, as He worked, as He rested, as He ate.

And Jesus gave this mission to the apostles and to us, but not to "go" as though ministry can only be done somewhere else. We are to share the good news as we "are going" through life—as we raise our children, as we shop, as we conduct our business, as we receive our education, as we travel on vacation. Yes, like the apostles before us, we are to carry out His mission as we go through the dailiness of life here and now, not later or after we go somewhere else.

Like the apostles, we are to carry out His mission as we go through the dailiness of life here and now, not later or after we go somewhere else.

Many of the apostles did "go" across the seas to other nations. And thank God they did so. But they didn't wait till they were somewhere else to begin the mission. They pursued it as they were going.

THE MESSAGE

Mark's story begins and ends with the term "gospel" or "good news" (Mark 1:1,14; 16:15). These occurrences are the only ones in the entire letter and they refer to the message that Jesus commissioned the apostles to take to the world. Framed by this good-news terminology is the good news itself.

The "news" is the story of Jesus. This sounds too simple. But how easy it is to preach response to the gospel as the gospel itself, and to assume that the news about Jesus is known. The news is so important that the New Testament contains four accounts. Let us make no assumptions. The response is faith, baptism and discipleship.

What makes the news "good" is the Resurrection. Some stories about heroic and compassionate men and women are fiction. They warm our hearts until we close the book and return to real life.

Other stories are true and factual. They move and inspire us to greater love and courage. But they also end like every other story, reminding us of our mortality.

Only the news about Jesus is truly good. Only His story has an ending we can *live* with. Paul puts it this way:

> Remember Jesus Christ, raised from the dead, descended from David. This is my gospel (2 Tim. 2:8).

No wonder so many responded in faith and baptism (Mark 16:16; Acts 2:41). The news was that good.

FOR REFLECTION

1. Define preaching.

2. How is "preaching" an act of worship?

3. Describe a ministry "as you are going."

4. Why did God choose preaching as the method of bringing salvation to the world?

5. Define "the gospel."

6. How have the forces of humanism and secularism affected preachers, audiences and the message?

7. What has been the impact of TV evangelism and the electronic Church on the message and the messengers?

8. Explain the meaning of resurrection for Christians today?

9. What accounts for the power that is in the Word of God?

10. What happens to our message when the story of Jesus is left out?